Contents

A Cub Scout Pack finds another country close to home

the 1988 CUB SCOUT annual

The Official Cub Scout Annual
of The Scout Association

Scouts

Edited by David Harwood

THE COVER PHOTOGRAPH
Cub Scouts go to interesting, unusual and exciting places! These three are looking over the huge aircraft fire engine at British Aerospace's Filton airfield.

THIS BOOK BELONGS TO

Published in Great Britain by
World International Publishing Limited.
An Egmont Company.
Egmont House, P.O. Box 111, Great Ducie Street,
Manchester M60 3BL.
Printed in Great Britain. ISBN 7235 6797 2

World

The Country Symbols Quiz

symbols devised and drawn by Vic Clapham

Our artist has drawn these symbols to represent sixteen countries of the world. In the bottom panel you will find the names of the countries.
Can you work out which symbol belongs to which country?

Answers on page 63

A VERY SPECIAL DAY

by Don Mackintosh

After London, the most popular place in Britain must surely be Windsor. Visitors from all over Britain and the world go to see the magnificent castle and the ancient cobbled streets.

But there is one particular day each year when Windsor has more visitors than on any other. It's the day when over 1,000 Queen's Scouts and their families attend the annual St. George's Day Parade and National Scout Service. For them, and for Windsor, it is a very special day.

The great privilege of parading in the Quadrangle at Windsor Castle, followed by the Service in St. George's Chapel in honour of Scouting's Patron Saint, was first granted by King George V in 1934.

A member of the Royal Family is nearly always there. Our present Queen has attended on several occasions, as have the Queen Mother, Princess Margaret and the Duke of Kent (who is President of The Scout Association). Scouts everywhere are very proud to be so honoured.

An early start

One day you may be one of the Queen's Scouts in the Parade. The day starts very early. It may even mean leaving home the day before, so you can be on time for the inspection and marching practice which take place on the Sunday morning.

"*That's* your left foot!" Queen's Scouts at marching practice with the Scots Guards before going on parade.

Super-smart. The Bournemouth Scout Band on the Quadrangle at Windsor Castle.

You will, of course, want to look your smartest in front of a member of the Royal Family and all the parents and other spectators who will be watching. First your uniform is checked to make sure that all badges are correct and in their right places. If something terrible has happened, like losing a button, helpers are on hand with needles and cotton!

Marching is not something Scouts do very often and keeping in step with other marchers can be difficult when you are not used to it. So, after inspection, everyone has the chance of some practice under the expert instruction of Drill Sergeants from a Guards Regiment.

It will probably surprise them, as well as you, to find that in little more than an hour, you have been turned into a presentable column of marchers!

After an early breakfast and all that exercise on the Barrack Square, you will be very hungry. So, off you go to lunch and possibly some sightseeing in the town. But don't go wandering off! You are due at the Royal Mews by 1.30 p.m.

Picture research by Maureen Downing

The Parade

In the Mews, the Queen's Scouts form in sections, each comprising a number of Counties or Areas. At the head of the Parade stands a Guards Band, resplendent in scarlet tunics and bearskins.

From now on everything is timed to the second.

On the command "Quick March" the Band strikes up and, with the Parade Leader and Colour Party at their head, the Queen's Scouts step out up the hill which leads to the Castle. Bringing up the rear is a splendidly turned out Scout Band. Entering the Castle Quadrangle through St. George's Gate, the Colour Party steps to one side while the main body of the Parade carries on to form two columns facing each other on both sides of the lawn.

All around the lawn the spectators are thronged. At the upper end between the Sovereign's Entrance, on the right, and the Equerry's Entrance, on the left, is a low platform which will be the Saluting Base.

A small party of Scout Gallantry Award holders waits outside the Equerry's Entrance while, by the Sovereign's Entrance, the Chief Scout and the Chief Executive Commissioner await the Royal visitor.

Meantime, with the Queen's Scouts all in position, the Parade Leader gives the order for the Colours to be brought on. The Parade comes to the "Alert" and the Colour Party marches up between the columns proudly bearing the King's Flag (so named after King George V who presented it to the Scouts), the Flag of St. George and The Scout Association Colour.

Then, suddenly, there *is* the Royal personage being greeted by the Chief Scout — exactly on time.

Mr Terry Bonfield who, as a boy was at B-P's first camp on Brownsea Island in 1907, joins two of today's Cub Scouts on the Windsor Castle lawn.

The Review and March Past

After the playing of the National Anthem, the Chief Scout invites the Royal visitor to review the Parade and, together with the Chief Executive Commissioner and a small army of press photographers, they tour the assembled columns, now and then pausing for a chat with some of those on parade. Meanwhile the crowd is entertained by music from the Guards Band and the Scout Band.

The Review ends when the Royal guest meets the Scout Gallantry Award holders outside the Equerry's Entrance and then returns to the Saluting Base for the March Past.

Once more the commands ring out and, led by the Scout Band and the Colour Party, the Parade marches past. As each section reaches the Saluting Base its leader salutes and gives the order "Eyes right". And so they march off out of the Quadrangle, through the crowd gathered outside, and take their places in St. George's Chapel ready for the National Scout Service.

"Eyes Right!" The Parade Leader and Colour Party salute HRH the Duke of Kent at the March Past.

Soldiers of the Queen. The Band of the Irish Guards marches off at the end of the Parade.

The National Scout Service

St. George's Chapel is large but packing in over 1,000 Queen's Scouts fills it from wall to wall. When they let themselves go on the hymns, the sound is really something and the crowds outside are able to join in because the Service is relayed to them by loudspeakers.

The Service is planned by Queen's Scouts and presided over by the Dean of Windsor. The Dean also gives the Address. There is a very special moment when, led by the Chief Scout, everyone stands to make the Scout Promise.

After the Service, the Queen's Scouts gather outside in the Horseshoe Cloister where the Chief Scout says a few words about the day. Then, with the Scout Band in the lead, they reform in columns and march back to the Royal Mews.

Gardening for Wildlife

written and illustrated
by Stephen Roberts

A GOOD BIRD TABLE

All gardens, large or small, have their share of wildlife. Some wildlife may be hard to see either because it comes to life only at night, or because it is too small to be seen with the naked eye. But, whatever the size of a garden, there are ways and means of attracting a greater variety of wildlife to it.

The most noticeable visitors to gardens are birds. Generally they visit for one reason only – food! The number of birds visiting your garden could be increased by the sort of food you put out for them.

Many kitchen scraps are suitable for birds: for example fat, cheese, brown bread (NOT white!), suet, bacon rind cut into small pieces, currants, apples, baked potatoes and stale cake. You can buy wild bird seed (which is a mixture of sunflower and millet seeds) and spread it on the ground for birds like chaffinches and greenfinches.

Throughout the year, but particularly in the cold winter months, try and provide water for our feathered friends. Birds must drink and bathe, and a very good way to provide both facilities is with a pond which has gently sloping sides, a few pond plants, and some rocks around the banks.

One very popular way of feeding birds in a garden is from a bird table. A basic bird table is a simple wooden tray (approximately 45 centimetres by 30 centimetres) with a 'lip' along each edge to prevent food being blown away. There is often a gap at each corner so the table can be easily cleaned, and to allow rain water to drain away. The Royal Society for the Protection of Birds produce a number of more substantial tables like the one illustrated here.

Food hoppers and baskets can be used to provide foods like peanuts which are much liked by blue tits and great tits.

A BLUE TIT AND A GREAT TIT FEEDING FROM A PEANUT BASKET

A MALE BRAMBLING FEEDING ON SEEDS IN THE SNOW

A BIRD BATH MADE FROM AN UPTURNED DUSTBIN LID

You can make a simple bird bath from an upturned dustbin lid supported by bricks and 'camouflaged' by plants.

Food and Shelter

If the search for food is one reason why birds visit gardens, shelter and a place to breed are two others. A variety of different bird boxes can be bought or built to provide birds like robins, blue tits, spotted flycatchers, redstarts and nuthatches with a home.

Many creatures eat the seeds and berries of plants. You could plant a few sunflowers in the spring and the seeding flower heads should attract greenfinches in the autumn. The seeds of thistles and groundsel will attract linnets and goldfinches. In the winter the berries of trees like holly, rowan and cotoneaster are eaten by blackbirds, redwings and thrushes.

Plants like ivy provide cover all year round for many birds and animals. Fruit bearing trees (e.g. apple, pear and cherry) provide food, and their blossom in the spring attracts insects.

Try and keep a corner of the garden a little wild and overgrown. Creatures like toads and slow worms prefer little crevices and holes.

The hedgehog is a welcome guest to gardens. It eats large quantities of slugs, millipedes and caterpillars. A saucer of milk and a slice of orange or tomato put out in the evening may attract one to your doorstep.

Butterflies make beautiful guests when encouraged by certain plants. Michaelmas daisies are liked by red admirals. The buddleia is often called 'the butterfly bush' because it attracts so many different species. The iceplant is irresistable to a whole host of insects.

ROBIN

NUTHATCH

HEDGEHOG

A YOUNG TOAD DOES NOT ALWAYS NEED TO BE NEAR WATER

A PEACOCK ON A BUDDLEIA

RED ADMIRAL

ROWAN BERRIES

SUNFLOWER

The Royal Society for the Protection of Birds is a national charity which works to protect and conserve Britain's birds and countryside. You can get further information about the RSPB, its publications and its products by writing to: RSPB, The Lodge, Sandy, Bedfordshire, SG19 2DL.

The Story of a Stamp

by David Harwood

photographs by
the Post Office and David Harwood

While Martin looked on, Keith signed the official visitors' book so he could be issued with a security pass.

On page 2 you can read how Keith Whitfield from Tyne and Wear won a competition to be the Cub Scout to 'star' in this feature. Keith travelled to London with his mother and his friend Martin Wolf and stayed overnight at Baden-Powell House, the Scouts' superb hostel in South Kensington. They had to get up early the next morning so we could catch the 08.25 train from Marylebone to High Wycombe in Buckinghamshire.

At High Wycombe we were met by chaffeur-driven cars and driven in style to Harrison and Sons, one of the world's leading security printers. As a security printer, Harrisons produce items which are worth much more than the paper on which they are printed like postage stamps, security documents, savings stamps, bonds and cheques.

The boys were welcomed by Derrick Howlett (Sales and Marketing Director) and John Harley (Administration Controller, Security Print Division). At reception we all had to sign the visitors' book, and were then issued with a special identification badge. With so much valuable 'paper' Harrisons cannot be too careful about who visits them and who works for them.

Now, in words and pictures you can read and see what the boys learnt and did during their very full and exciting day.

This was a particularly special moment during the visit. While chatting to one of Harrisons retouchers, the boys were able to have a close look at the original artwork of the barn owl, painted by artist Ken Lilley, for the conservation stamps issued in 1986.

The birth of a stamp

In Britain there are two main types of stamp. The definitives are those stamps with the Queen's profile as the only feature. Each value has its own colour and as they have no fixed 'life', they will be printed again and again for a long period of time. The other stamps are the special issues or commemoratives which are on sale for a relatively short time. About eight different sets of commemoratives are issued each year.

Work on a special or commemorative issue usually starts at least two years before you can actually buy it from a Post Office. (There are exceptions, however, like

the stamp which was issued to mark the wedding of Prince Andrew and Sarah Ferguson in 1986. That stamp was produced in eight weeks.)

So where does the story of a stamp begin? First, the Marketing Department of the Post Office goes through hundreds of ideas for subjects for a particular year. These ideas come from various organisations, the public and the government as well as those suggested by the Post Office's own research. They are looking for ways of celebrating national and international events, telling interesting stories about Britain and its people and marking important anniversaries.

All the ideas are discussed by the Stamp advisory Committee which includes Post Office staff and people representing design, philately and public opinion. The Committee puts suggestions to the Post Office Board which makes the final decision for the themes of the issues for a calendar year.

Royal approval

Next, top artists and designers are asked to produce ideas for a particular stamp or set of stamps. Generally three different approaches by three different artists are tried for each subject.

The artist first does a drawing at actual stamp size to make sure that his idea will work. The Stamp Advisory Committee considers the artists' ideas and chooses one to produce the artwork for the actual stamp or set of stamps.

The artists and Post Office design team research the subject very carefully to make sure everything is accurate in every detail. For example, Alex Jardine, who was the artist for the British River Fish stamps, kept some fish in his bath at home so his illustrations could be in living colour!

The final artwork is usually produced four times larger than stamp size and, when the finishing touches have been completed, it is sent to the printers for sets of colour proofs, known as essays, to be made.

These essays are approved by the Stamp Advisory Committee, and submitted to Buckingham Palace for the Queen's personal approval. They are looked at very carefully, and the Queen has been known to suggest changes.

As soon as Royal approval has been granted, the artwork goes into a production programme with the printer.

Paper, gum and ink

Many things have to be taken into account when printing stamps, particularly at Harrisons because the firm produces stamps for more than 100 countries and supplies the high quality gummed and coated paper for stamps for about 160 countries.

Countries with different climates have different needs for their stamps. The make-up of the paper, the coating, the gum and the printing inks are all things which have to be considered. For example, as gum absorbs moisture more quickly than paper, it is important to use the correct gum for countries with humid climates, otherwise the sheets of printed stamps would stick together and be useless.

One view of the huge paper coating machine. Each reel of paper is worth about £500 before any stamps are printed on it! The reel at the top left of the picture is about to automatically attach itself to the end of the reel running though the machine. The next reel is ready on the fork lift truck.

THE STAMP PRINTERS

Harrison & Sons was founded in 1750. The company received its first stamp contract from the Post Office in 1881, but since 1934 it has had a non-stop contract, producing about 5,000 million stamps a year.

The Post Office also uses two other large printing firms for its stamp production – Waddingtons and the House of Questa. Unlike Harrisons these firms specialise in a different printing process called offset lithography. Each year one special stamp issue is produced by this method and the two firms also receive contracts to print some low value definitives.

The work of an engraver demands tremendous skill, patience and an eye for minute detail. Here an engraver is working on a cylinder which will be used to print definitive stamps. The cylinder has been faced with chrome to reduce the wear on the printing machine's doctor blade. You can see the engraver's box of tools in the left foreground.

Keith and Martin watching the world's largest and fastest stamp printing machine in operation.

Harrisons' Sales and Marketing Director Derrick Howlett showing the boys how the printed sheets of stamps are checked when they come off the presses. The coloured strips on the wall at the back are the basic colours of inks used for stamp printing.

The paper for the stamps is run through a machine which adds a chalk-based coating to one side to ensure a good printing surface and so that the colours used by the artist are exactly reproduced. Organic phosphor (which is derived from granite) is often included in the coating for British stamps because it is this substance which will be picked up by the Post Office's machinery which arranges letters so they all face the same way, and then automatically sorts letters into First Class and Second Class mail.

The coated paper is then run through another machine which puts gum on the non-coated side. The gum used for British stamps nowadays is naturally clear, and a pale blue dye is added so people can see it is there.

The paper is now ready for printing.

Definitive British stamps are printed in one colour, but commemorative stamps usually have several colours. The printer first decides how many primary colours he needs to combine with the white of the coated paper to exactly reproduce the artist's original painting. The artist – and the printer – have to be careful that darker colours do not cover the paper so thickly that the phosphor in the coating cannot be 'read' by the facing and sorting machines.

Colour, cylinders and cells

Almost all British stamps produced by Harrisons use the photogravure printing process. Until Harrisons pioneered photogravure for printing stamps in bulk, the process was used mainly for reproducing fine works of art.

In photogravure printing, a copper cylinder is prepared for each colour used. A cylinder has 400 identical stamp images for definitives or 200 for the larger commemoratives. Each image is made up of

STAMPS WITHOUT A NAME

Britain is the only country in the world which never puts its name on its stamps. When the world's first postage stamps were printed in the United Kingdom in 1840 they carried only a portrait of Queen Victoria on them. It was assumed that everyone around the world who received a letter with a stamp on it would know where it had come from! That tradition has continued ever since, both on definitive stamps, where the monarch's head is full of detail, and on special or commemorative stamps where the profile is quite small.

Keith and Martin were amazed at the speed with which the highly trained checkers flicked through the piles of printed stamp sheets. A checker can spot an error the size of a pin head! And considering that Harrisons print a total of 5,000 million stamps a year, that's an awful lot of checking!

During a break in their full day, Keith and Martin were entertained to a magnificent buffet lunch in the board room. At the end of their visit, Mr. Howlett presented them with a number of stamps, booklets and a special magnifying glass to study their own stamps when they got home.

thousands of tiny cells etched into the surface of the cylinder. There are 50,000 cells to each square inch.

In a complex process, corrosive acids are used to etch – or 'eat away' – cells to varying depths in the copper surface. The deepest is 1.5/1000 of an inch and the shallowest 0.5/1000 of an inch. The deeper the cell, the more ink a cell will hold and therefore the darker the tone of the colour.

Although computerised machinery helps the process, sometimes only the traditional skills and craftsmanship of the etcher and the engraver, working by hand, can produce the perfect result.

When cylinders have been patiently and painstakingly checked, image by image, cell by cell, the presses are prepared and the printing of the stamps can begin. The stamp paper is pressed against each colour cylinder in turn, 'absorbing' the printing ink held in the cells. When running at full speed, Harrisons machines will print and perforate up to 15,000 sheets of stamps an hour.

At every stage the stamps are checked by staff from both Harrisons and the Post Office for quality and quantity. They are then packed very carefully and securely.

So the next time you stick a stamp on a letter just think how much time, care and skill has gone into its production. Every stamp is a miniature masterpiece!

ACKNOWLEDGEMENTS

The CUB SCOUT ANNUAL is most grateful to the Post Office for sponsoring and making all the arrangements for this visit. We would also like to thank Harrison and Sons (particularly Derrick Howlett) for their co-operation and generous hospitality.

THE ROYAL WEDDING 1986

The marriage of Prince Andrew and Miss Sarah Ferguson was marked by two special stamps issued by the Post Office on the day before the Royal Wedding on 22 July 1986. The designer Jeffrey Matthews gave the stamps a distinctive touch by using Prince Andrew's Royal Navy insignia on the 17p value with a complementary design of wedding bells on the 12p value.

ROYAL VISIT

Harrisons were privileged and proud to have had a private royal visit to their High Wycombe factory by Prince Andrew and Miss Sarah Ferguson on 9 June 1986 when they saw 'their' stamp being produced.

Codebreaker!

This message is written in code. Can you crack the code and read the message? It may seem an odd message, but it's unusual because all the 26 letters in the alphabet have been used (some more than once). The long single vertical lines show a break between letters, and the double vertical lines show a break between words.

If you think you've found the key, check your answer on page 58.

If you're stuck, here's a clue . . . look at the numbers on your digital watch or calculator.

If you still cannot crack the code, turn to page 27 for a further clue.

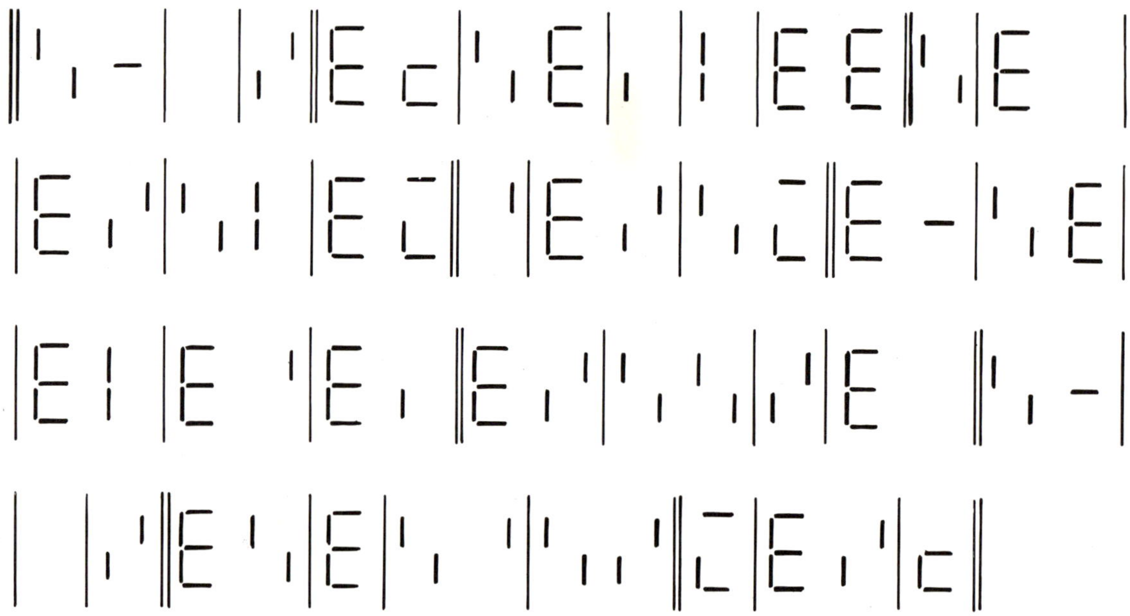

TITCH . . . Cub Scout

by Leslie Cecil

THE STAR

by Hazel Addis
illustrated by Mark Viney

Long, long ago and far, far away there lived a shepherd's boy called Mark. His father was the head shepherd who looked after hundreds of sheep.

Ever since he was five, Mark had wanted to be a shepherd but he was always told he was too young. The men would go out with the flock for days and nights at a time, watching over the sheep while they grazed. There were wolves in the woods nearby, which might sneak out and grab a helpless little lamb when its mother wasn't looking. So the shepherds had to be always on the watch.

At last, Mark was eight. For his birthday his dad gave him a real shepherd's crook, cut down to size, and his mum gave him a long woollen robe with orange and brown stripes, which she had woven for him. So then, as a proper shepherd, Mark set off with the others next day, driving the sheep up the long grassy slopes to the distant hills.

At night, the men sat round a bonfire, talking and laughing, and taking turns to sleep, while the others kept watch. One night, when it seemed extra dark and cold, something very extraordinary happened.

It was Christmas Eve, but nobody knew that because, in those days, there was no Christmas. It was nearly 2,000 years ago.

Mark was tired and glad that it was his turn to sleep first. So, immediately after their supper of bread and cheese, he curled up in his orange-striped robe and fell asleep at once. He had wonderful dreams, full of glowing light and people singing, when suddenly he was woken by his father's hand on his shoulder.

Mark sat up slowly, trying to blink the sleep from his eyes. "Is it my turn already?" he asked.

"No," said his father. "But something has happened and we have to go."

"Go? What do you mean, Dad? Go where? Why?"

"Hush, my son," said his dad gently. "We have seen a vision and heard the voice of an angel calling us, and we must go."

Mark began to think he was still dreaming. The clouds still seemed to be glowing with light and echoing with the sound of those voices singing. "I don't understand," he said. "What did the angel say?"

Several shepherds told him that they didn't understand either, they had been too scared to listen. It was Dad who explained. He told Mark that Christ the Lord had been born. Then, putting his arm round Mark's shoulder, he pointed, saying, "Look!"

Mark looked up and saw the most enormous star shining in the night sky away to the east. Everything seemed to be touched with silver.

"What – what does it mean?" he whispered.

"It is a sign from God, marking the place," his father answered. "We must go and see it for ourselves."

"Can I come too?" asked Mark, wide awake now.

"No, son, it may be a long way – too far for you. Besides, we cannot all leave the flock. Can you look after them while we are gone?"

For a moment Mark was terrified. Then, looking up at the star, he suddenly felt big and strong and said, "Yes, Dad. We'll be all right."

The men were soon off, Mark's father only pausing to call back, "Fear not! We'll all be safe." Mark watched the tall figures striding away into the darkness towards the east.

Then – he was alone.

He threw more wood on the fire to make it blaze up. He squatted beside it, knowing he must not go to sleep again. He was head shepherd now.

Once he heard a wolf howling, and he went walking among the sheep, talking to them, telling them that everything was all right.

But he was very nearly asleep when he heard a strange sound. Jumping up, he saw a big, dark shadow coming up behind him. He snatched a blazing branch from the fire to frighten it away. But it came nearer and nearer, and suddenly a voice called, "It's all right, boy!"

It was a man riding a camel, which many people did in those days. He was leading a little donkey, laden down with bags of luggage. "Where is the head shepherd?" the man demanded.

"I am the only shepherd here," answered Mark. "Can I help you, sir?"

"We are thirsty," said the stranger.

Mark pointed to the rough trough where the sheep drank, saying, "You are welcome."

He was a very grand-looking man, with brightly-coloured robes and jewels flashing in the light from the star. Perhaps he was a lord, or a prince from some faraway land. The donkey looked tired and Mark patted him as he drank.

The man was smiling. "Tell me, boy, what town lies yonder?" and he pointed to the east.

"There's a little place called Bethlehem not far away," said Mark. "I don't know what's beyond that."

"Is there a way across these hills?"

"Yes, sir. My father and the shepherds went off that way not long ago."

"Why?" asked the great man.

Mark couldn't really explain, so he pointed to the star and said, "Because of that."

"That is why I am going, too," said the prince. "For years I have studied the heavens, but I have never seen anything like that before."

"My dad said it was a sign from God."

"He is a wise man," the prince nodded, adding, "wouldn't you like to see this great thing, too? You can ride the donkey and come with me."

Mark looked at the donkey, thinking what fun it would be. The donkey looked at him sadly. "No thank you, sir," said Mark, "I must stay and look after the flock."

"You are a good shepherd," said the prince, and rode off into the darkness leaving Mark alone again, except for the sheep and the star.

Next evening, the shepherds came back. They were very tired and thirsty, but there was a shiny look on their faces. As they all ate their supper round the fire, they told Mark an extraordinary story about a baby born in a stable and lying in a manger, and yet everybody knew that he was a King of Kings.

"But kings are born in palaces!" Mark protested, "Not stables."

"This is no ordinary king," he was told. "This is the Lord."

"But Lord of what? King of where?"

"The Lord of all mankind," his father explained.

Mark was longing to tell them about his adventure with the prince on the camel but it didn't seem so important now and his dad was saying, "You have done well, Mark, and I am proud of you. You shall sleep all night, and tomorrow we take the flock home."

But, tired as he was, Mark didn't sleep all night. He was woken by the sound of voices and one of them was the voice of the prince. Sitting up, Mark saw the shepherds gathered round bowing to the great man.

"Did I not see you in Bethlehem?" the prince was asking.

"Yes, my lord. We were there."

"Then blessed are we all," said the stranger. "But where is the boy? Sleeping, as he deserves?"

"No, I'm here!" cried Mark, running forward.

"This is my son, Mark," his father explained.

"We are old friends," smiled the prince, while the shepherds stared in amazement. "And I'd like to repay him for his kindness," the man went on. "Mark, my donkey is too tired to go any further. He was carrying gold and presents for the Christ child and now his work is done. Will you keep him and care for him?"

Mark couldn't even say thank you – he just put his arms round the little donkey's neck and hugged him.

"Farewell, my friends," said the prince. "The star has faded from the sky, but may it never fade from our hearts." And with that, he was gone.

Next day, they drove the flock down the hills towards home, Mark leading the way, riding his own little donkey.

You may think that is the end of the story, but it's not. It is only a little bit of the beginning of a story which has gone on ever since. It is the story of Christmas.

RAPTOR RESCUE

As well as running a Branch of Raptor Rescue, Mr Doughty has trained some birds of prey. He is an expert falconer, and hunts this lanner falcon in the countryside around his home. Here Mr Doughty's falcon shows off its long tapered wings which are perfect for fast flight.

written and photographed by Michael Edwards

Two large orange owl eyes followed my every move as I walked up a garden path in the Lincolnshire village of South Willingham. Then, the loud 'kee, kee, kee' call of a kestrel cried across the lawn. I knew I had the right address. In that neighbourhood, only ten-year-old Andrew Mott's garden had falcons, hawks and owls rather than blue tits, sparrows and starlings.

You see, Andrew's parents, Martin and Diana Doughty, run Raptor Rescue, which is a service dedicated to saving sick and injured birds of prey.

Mr Doughty, who is head teacher of a local school, has been with Raptor Rescue, a national charity, since 1984, although he has been caring for sick birds for fifteen years.

"We have been made more aware of sick and injured birds of prey dying because no one seems to know what to do with them," Mr Doughty told me. "We believe that more birds of prey can

Andrew proudly holds the Portman Building Society's bronze sparrowhawk trophy which he won in the 1985 Cub Scout Annual Nature Roundabout Competition. The real sparrowhawk on his left hand is one which he is helping his father nurse back to health.

Mr Doughty treats a long-eared owl which had flown into overhead electric cables. Its left wing was so badly damaged that it had to be amputated.

This short-eared owl, still frightened from its ordeal of being shot, took eight days before it would feed itself.

Almost all birds have good eyesight, but birds of prey have the best vision. They can see many times better than Man. Look at the size of this lanner falcon's eye.

be saved and released back into the wild if correct and immediate care is given. It's far better for someone who knows something about birds of prey to look after them, rather than trying to put things right yourself."

The Doughty's freezer is stocked with raptorial goodies like mice, rabbits and birds, many of which they get from a local game supplier. Vitamins are added to the food to keep the birds in good condition. Young birds are given calcium to strengthen their bones and assist feather growth.

In 1985 thirty-eight birds came in for treatment. When I visited, nine were still captive due to serious injury, fourteen had been successfully released back into the wild, and fifteen had died. Mr Doughty told me that many more birds would have died if Duguid, Murdoe and Startup, a veterinary practice in Lincoln, hadn't helped. "They are really marvellous. They treat our birds free of charge and we are very grateful to them. Operations on birds are very expensive, and we just couldn't afford to pay."

"We would like to think that the service we offer through Raptor Rescue is doing some good," said Mr Doughty. "We are getting birds back into their own environment."

Mr Doughty bought this common buzzard for hunting. He also takes it to schools and country shows when he tells people about the work of Raptor Rescue. Notice how the buzzard puts out its feet before alighting on Mr Doughty's hand, which is protected from the bird's strong talons by a strong glove called a gauntlet. The leather straps around the bird's legs are called jesses.

COLOUR

The world around us is full of colour. Colour can make things bright or dull. We become used to things being particular colours. Would you enjoy pink eggs? Or green sky? Or blue milk?

Colour is often associated with emotion and feelings. We say people are 'red with anger', 'blue with cold', 'green with envy'.

Colours are used to explain or identify things. For example, traffic signs have different colours for different purposes. Signs with red borders are warnings, signs with blue backgrounds give information and signs with green backgrounds give directions.

We see colour because light shines on things. Sunlight appears white, but it contains all the colours of the 'spectrum'. If you shine white light though a glass prism, the path of light is bent, and because some colours bend more than others, the colours separate and appear as the 'spectrum' . . .

RED, ORANGE, YELLOW, GREEN, BLUE, INDIGO, VIOLET.

The change from red to violet is gradual, but we usually talk about these seven colours as being the visible 'spectrum'.

Rain can bend the path of sunlight, too. This is how we see a rainbow. The raindrops have the same effect as a prism on the rays of light.

Some people see two colours as the same. For example, a person may not be able to distinguish red and green. These people are colour blind. Not many people are colour blind, but each person probably sees colours in a slightly different way.

Here is something you can make to show how the colours of the spectrum make white, and the effect of the rainbow.

1

Cut a circle approximately 14 cm in diameter from a piece of fairly thick white card.

2

Divide one side into *six* equal segments (the angle of each segment at the centre will be 60°). Colour in the segments as shown.

3

Divide the second side into *four* equal segments (quarters, so the angle of each segment at the centre will be 90°). In two opposite quarters, draw the arcs of six circles as shown. The inner arc should have a radius of 1 cm, the next a radius of 2 cm, the third 3 cm, and so on. Colour in the arcs, as shown.

4

In each of the other two quarters on the second side, pierce a hole about 1 cm out from the centre of the circle.

5

Thread string through, as shown, and join the ends of the string in a reef knot.

6

Move the cardboard circle to the middle of the string. Hold the loops at each end and spin the disc towards you to 'wind up' the string. Then pull hands apart and the card will start to spin in the opposite direction. To keep the disc spinning, slacken your 'pull' before the string completely unwinds, so it can 'wind up' in the other direction. Repeat to keep the disc spinning. With a bit of practice, you'll quickly become an expert spinner!
When the disc is spinning, one side should appear almost white . . . if your colours are correct! The second side should appear as a rainbow.
When you've successfully operated this spinner, you could try making circles with different patterns and colours.

devised and drawn by Malcolm Turner

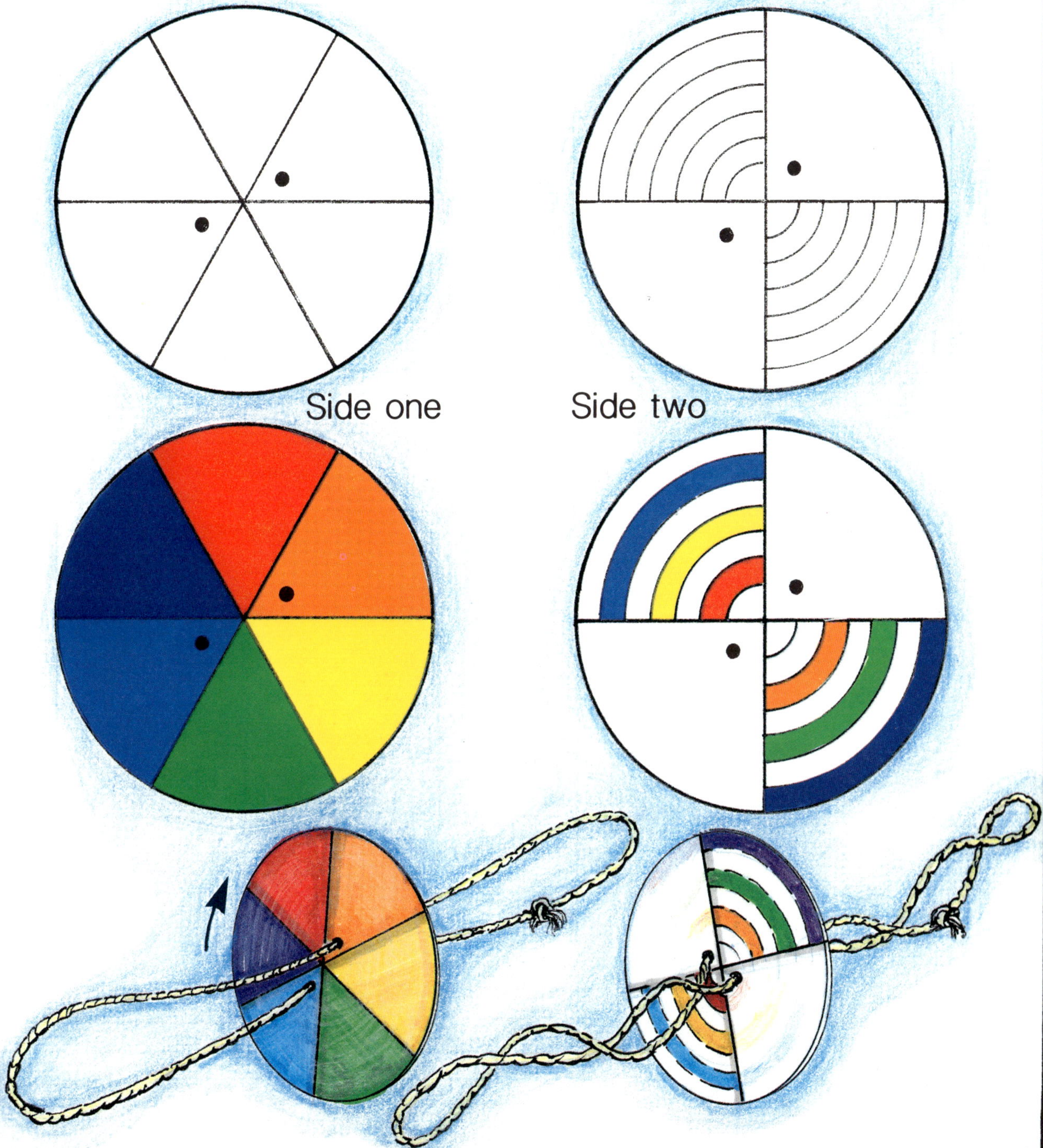

PROFICIENCY PUZZLE PAGE

RHYMING PUZZLE IF YOU HOLD THE BOOK READER BADGE, THIS ONE SHOULD BE EASY! ALL YOU HAVE TO DO IS FIND FOUR FACIAL FEATURES AND FOUR ARTICLES OF CLOTHING ABOUT THIS LAD THAT RHYME WITH THE PICTURES AROUND HIM.

WHICH PROFICIENCY BADGE? COLOUR IN ALL THE SHAPES WITH A DOT. WHICH PROFICIENCY BADGE IS SUGGESTED?

STOLEN SPORTS THIEVES BROKE INTO THE PACK'S STORES AND STOLE ALL THEIR SPORTS GEAR. BUT THE CUBS DISTURBED THE BURGLARS, WHO RUSHED OFF THROUGH THE WOODS THROWING THE GEAR ALL OVER THE PLACE. SEE IF YOU CAN FIND THEIR EQUIPMENT FOR THEM. (THERE MIGHT BE MORE THAN ONE OF EACH!) WHAT GAMES COULD THEY HAVE PLAYED?

SOLUTIONS ON PAGE 63

Day Trip to Africa

written and photographed by Ron Jeffries

When the 1st Ilford Cub Scout Pack set off for their annual camp, each Cub Scout was given a programme booklet. It told them about the exciting activities they would enjoy during the weekend. Imagine their surprise when they read through the booklet and discovered that on the Saturday morning they would be leaving for a trip to Africa!

The Pack was camping at Hargreaves Camp Site and Activity Centre in Essex, and if some of the Cub Scouts expected to fly to Africa from London's Heathrow Airport, they were in for another surprise because a coach arrived for them.

In the coach Akela explained that they would be driving to the village of Takeley, near Bishops Stortford in Hertfordshire, where they would go to Aklowa, the African traditional heritage village. At the village they would meet Felix Cobbson (the Founder-Director of Aklowa) and a group of Ghanaians who would introduce them to African cooking, drumming and canoeing.

Ghana is a country in West Africa. Its capital city is Accra. The people living in that part of Ghana are of the Ga tribe, and 'Aklowa' means 'village' in the Ga language.

When the 1st Ilford Cub Scouts (who wear blue scarves) arrived at Aklowa they were joined by their friends from the 2nd Seven Kings Pack (wearing red and black scarves).

The picture at the top of this page shows the Cub Scouts enjoying a feast at the end of their day trip to Africa. They are eating peanuts roasted in sand, maize fritters, salad and freshly-made fruit juice. On the next page you can see some more of the exciting things these Cubs did at Aklowa.

On arrival at Aklowa, the Cub Scouts met Founder-Director Felix Cobbson. Felix explained that his group is called the Aklowa Drummers and Dancers (the Village Drummers and Dancers) because it is in the villages of Ghana where the traditional activities are to be found.

'If you live in a house built with bricks and a thatched roof, what do you call it?' Felix asked the Cub Scouts.

'A thatched cottage,' they replied.

'And if I live in a house with mud walls and a straw roof, what do you call that?' Felix enquired.

'A mud hut,' replied the Cubs.

'But surely,' said Felix, 'the bricks in your house are made from mud, and the thatch is straw! Why call your house a thatched cottage, and mine a mud hut?'

And so the Cub Scouts were divided into three groups and went off to see Aklowa's thatched cottages . . .

With one of Aklowa's thatched cottages in the background, this group of Cub Scouts learned that before you can cook delicious fritters you have to grind the maize into flour. They all lent a hand, using the long wooden pole to grind the seeds. They managed to keep most of the seeds in the wooden bowl, but it's not as easy as it looks.

When the maize had been ground into flour, the Cub Scouts watched as the small balls of dough were rubbed out on a board and then dropped into hot fat to fry. Then the Cub Scouts tried cooking the fritters for themselves. Notice how the wood for the fire has been placed on the ground in a star shape. As the logs burned away at one end, the Cubs pushed the unburnt end towards the centre to keep a steady heat below the cooking pan. The Cubs also roasted peanuts the African way! You can see them doing this in the photo on page 3. The shallow bowl was first warmed over the fire, and then some clean sand was heated in the bottom of the pan. Next, freshly shelled peanuts were placed in the sand, and then stirred with a wooden spoon. The sand and peanuts had to be stirred constantly while they were over the fire, otherwise the nuts would have quickly burnt. When the peanuts were cooked through, the sand was shaken off through a fine-mesh sieve and the peanuts eaten hot. Delicious!

The Cub Scouts went into a big house near the African village to play the drums. The Cubs were told that the drums were not called tom-toms because each drum made its own sound, just like the different instruments in an orchestra.

The drums you can see in this photograph are Fontomfrom Drums, which are the pride of the Akan people of Ghana. The drums are very heavy and are carried on the heads of bearers during ceremonial processions: the drummers walk behind and play the drums with sticks which are bent back at one end. The Fontomfrom Drums produce a very deep and penetrating sound.

There were a dozen or so different types of drum for the Cub Scouts to play, and within half an hour they *were* playing music!

Working in pairs, the Cub Scouts tried canoeing the African way. The dug-out canoes were steered around the lagoon by using the paddles on one side or the other, depending on which way the 'crew' wanted their canoe to go. In the background you can see the rest of the Cubs waiting to have a go, with the African village in the distance.

The Cub Scouts are enjoying Ghanaian food at the end of their day trip to Africa. The bowls and spoons were not traditional African design but plastic. The food was highly spiced ... enjoyed by some, but others were not so sure!

As these Cub Scouts discovered, the really great thing about the visit was that they didn't just stand and watch and stare, but they actually took part.

I'm a Cub Scout because...

. . . of the adventure from camping to sports, and the enjoyment from earning badges.

LEE BLACK

3rd Enfield Cub Scout Pack, Middlesex

. . . I like to help other people and to keep the Cub Scout Law. I used to collect pictures of Lord Robert Baden-Powell.

FAYAAZ MOOSA

Red Cub Scout Pack, Bulawayo, Zimbabwe

. . . we do lots of exciting things together all year round. We never have time to get bored. We learn about things that you do not learn at school or home.

RICKIE BOWLER

Austin Cub Scout Pack, Northwingfield, Derbyshire

illustrations by Malcolm Turner

For the 1986 CUB SCOUT ANNUAL Challenge we asked you, the readers, to complete the sentence 'I'm a Cub Scout because . . .' in not more than 30 words.

There were lots of entries. We would like to thank all of you who had a go. Unfortunately we do not have enough room to print them all, so we have had to make a selection. The writer of each one chosen has received a free copy of this 1988 Annual.

There's another Cub Scout Annual Challenge this year. The details are on page 62. Why don't YOU send in an entry?

. . . I like mixing with other boys, joining in the activities, and learning new skills. I find it very interesting learning about Cubs from other countries.

STEVEN MOORE

Redcliff's Cub Scout Pack, Christchurch, New Zealand

. . . I like playing games and exercise and doing first aid. I like going to fund raising events to buy stuff.

EVAN LAMBERT

1st Strathaven 'D' Cub Scout Pack, Lanarkshire, Scotland

. . . I like my Akela and I like going camping and other things like that.

IDRIS DAVIES

Tutong English Cub Scout Pack, Brunei

. . . my brother was a Cub and he enjoyed himself going camping and making things, and I thought that's what I'd like to do.

JAMES COE

1st Claydon Cub Scout Pack, Suffolk

I'm a Cub Scout because . . . it's fun:
Camping, craftwork, good turns done.
Road safety, home safety, pantomimes;
Great games, new friends, happy times.
Beavers 'Goodbye', Cubs 'Hello!' –
After Cubs, to Scouts I'll go!

JOHN ANTHONY GREER

Holywood, County Down, Northern Ireland

. . . it is a great family to belong to. I hope I might become a Queen's Scout like my cousins are. My mum, nan, aunties and girl cousins have all been Guides.

MATTHEW STANLEY

1st Walton-on-Thames Cub Scout Pack, Surrey

. . . my friends are Cubs and they told me about it. It sounded exciting so as soon as I was eight, I became a Cub.

IAN BENNETT

1st Thornbury (Mohawk) Cub Scout Pack, Avon

. . . I like going to my Pack Meeting every week. There is always something interesting to do, and new to learn with my other Cub friends.

MATTHEW PRICE

18th Lincoln (Bailgate) Cub Scout Pack, Lincolnshire

. . . it is good because we play lots of games, do Job Week, help old people, and go on outings, camps and nature rambles. And we do Arrow work.

DEREK BAILLIE

1st Kyle/21st Rosshire Cub Scout Pack, Scotland

. . . I get the chance to do new and exciting things that I would not normally be able to do.

SIMON GRICE

12th Doncaster/1st Bawtry Cub Scout Pack, South Yorkshire

. . . I enjoy all the activities. We have lots of fun and do interesting Arrow work. I think being a Cub makes me a better person.

MATTHEW LINGARD

Stowbridge, West Midlands

. . . of all the different things Cubs do like team games, badge work, camping and helping others. Best of all I like being in the Gang Show, and competing in District competitions.

MATTHEW CROSSLEY

36th Blackpool Cub Scout Pack, Lancashire

. . . I like football, doing badge work and playing games. You learn how to help other people and to look after yourself.

SIMON McKINLEY

114th Dunfirmline Cub Scout Pack, Fife, Scotland

. . . I like going camping and playing football. I like entering competitions, and I like working for badges.

DAVID GALE

19th Maidenhead Cub Scout Pack, Berkshire

CODEBREAKER CLUE

IF YOU'VE NOT TRIED THE CODED MESSAGE ON PAGE 14 YET, TURN BACK AND HAVE A GO FIRST! Here's a big clue to help you break the coded message:

|| 20 | 8 | 5 || 17 | 21 | 9 | 3 | 11 || 2 | 18 |

| 15 | 23 | 14 || 6 | 15 | 24 || 10 | 21 |

| 13 | 16 | 19 || 15 | 22 | 5 | 18 || 20 |

| 8 | 5 || 12 | 1 | 26 | 25 || 4 | 15 | 7 ||

Don't forget there are 26 letters in the alphabet!

If you're still puzzled, turn to page 58 and all will be revealed!

Some ideas for THINGS TO MAKE

by Vic Clapham

PLASTER LEAF CASTS

You will need:
- the lid of a tin or a plastic container
- petroleum jelly
- an eyelet
- plaster of Paris
- paint

1. Make a nick in the lid to take a screw-type eyelet as shown in the sketch.
2. Using a piece of soft cloth, coat the inside of the lid with a thin film of petroleum jelly.
3. Coat the *underside* of the leaf with a very thin film of petroleum jelly.
4. Place the eyelet in position in the lid (as illustrated). Mix plaster of Paris powder with water to a thick, creamy consistency. Pour the mixture into the lid until it is full, making sure that the eyelet is well embedded.
5. After a few minutes, when the plaster has set slightly but is still soft, place the leaf in the centre of the plaster with its underside down and the point of the leaf in line with the eyelet. Press the leaf lightly so it makes a clear impression in the plaster.
6. When the plaster is reasonably dry, carefully peel off the leaf.
7. Turn the lid upside-down and carefully tap the plaster cast out of the lid.
8. Allow the cast to dry overnight. Then, wiping the leaf impression to remove all traces of the petroleum jelly, paint the leaf impression in its natural colour(s) with water colour, poster colour or enamel paint.

PAPER BEADS

You will need:
- coloured paper
- glue
- a few old thin knitting needles
- clear varnish
- strong thread or nylon line

You can make attractive beads from strips of coloured paper. You can use leftover wallpaper, colour pages from magazines, etc.

1. Cut the coloured paper into strips about 30 cm long. Depending on the size of the bead you want to make, the width can be from 2 cm to as wide as you like. By cutting the ends of the strips in different shapes you can produce different shaped beads (see illustration).

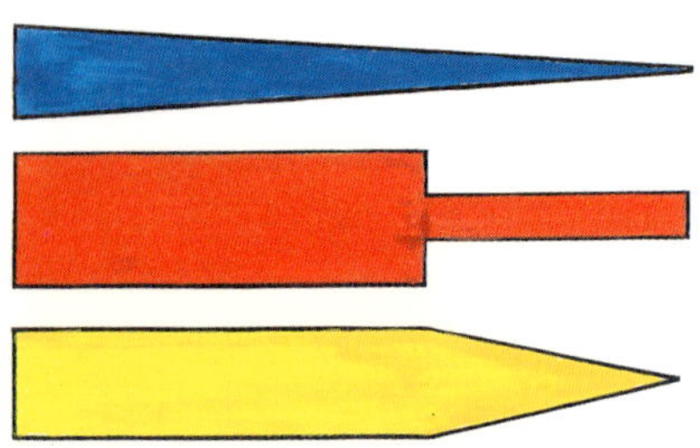

TYPICAL SHAPES OF COLOURED PAPER STRIPS, FOR MAKING PAPER BEADS.

2. To make a bead:
   a. lay a paper strip, coloured side down, on sheets of scrap paper.
   b. spread glue or paste over the upper facing surface of the strip.
   c. form the bead by rolling the strip tightly from the *wide* end around the thin knitting needle. Make sure the end is well pasted down before sliding the bead off the needle.
   d. leave the completed beads to dry overnight.
   e. when they are completely dry, carefully paint them with clear varnish.
   f. when the varnish is dry, string the beads on strong thread or nylon line to make an attractive necklace as a present.
3. Make a few experimental beads first. Then, when you have chosen the sizes and shapes of bead that you like, you can make cardboard templates to the shapes you need. Use the templates for marking out the strips so that each bead in a 'series' will be exactly the same size and shape.

You can also make bead bracelets or even belts. Large paper beads, 6 cm to 9 cm wide, can be used to make decorative curtains when strung from a wooden rod.

PLASTER CARVING BLOCKS

You will need:
- small cardboard box or waxed carton
- petroleum jelly
- plaster of Paris
- old tin or plastic container

1. Find a small cardboard box or waxed carton that's roughly the shape and size as the subject you wish to carve. Milk and fruit juice cartons are ideal.
2. If you're using a cardboard box you'll need to smear petroleum jelly very thinly over the inside of the box. If you use a waxed carton you will NOT need to use petroleum jelly.
3. Mix plaster of Paris with water in an old container to get a fairly thick, smooth mixture.
4. Pour the mixture into the box.
5. Let the plaster dry and harden for at least eight hours.

6. Carefully remove the box or carton and you have a splendid plaster carving block. Leave it for a few more hours to harden completely.
7. Put plenty of old newspapers or an old plastic tablecloth on the surface on which you're going to work to avoid making a mess.
8. Carve away with a penknife or modelling knife, BUT REMEMBER TO BE VERY CAREFUL WHEN USING SHARP TOOLS.

LEAF PICTURES

You will need:
- a picture frame
- stiff mounting paper
- card
- glue

1. If you do not have an empty photo or picture frame, try and find an old frame which you can clean up and possibly paint to look like new.
2. Cut a piece of stiff paper for mounting your leaves or grasses to the same size as the glass. Cartridge paper, which may be tinted or textured, is ideal for mounting.
3. Cut a piece of strong backing card, also the same size as the glass.
4. Collect the leaves and/or grasses which you wish to mount. It is best to use green leaves. You can use autumn leaves, but these tend to be brittle and can break easily. Grasses are best picked when dry.
5. Place your collection between several sheets of newspaper, and put a pile of books or other suitable weights on top to press them.
6. Leave them to dry thoroughly for about three weeks.
7. Arrange the leaves or grasses on the mounting paper, moving them around until you have an attractive arrangement. As shown in the illustration, the use of a large leaf spray in the centre is a good way to start. Grasses are usually best arranged in a bunch or spray.

8. When you are satisfied with your arrangement, carefully stick down each leaf with rubber solution or clear glue or adhesive: you will only need a light touch of glue here and there.
9. Polish the glass before putting the frame back together. Hang your picture on a wall out of the sunlight because the leaves will tend to fade in strong sunlight.

LEAF AND GRASS PICTURES MAKE VERY ATTRACTIVE PRESENTS!

BIRD FEATHER COLLECTION

You can learn a lot about birds by collecting their feathers. You can often find feathers in the garden, the fields and the woods and along the banks of rivers, lakes and ponds.

You will be able to identify some feathers yourself. For those you cannot identify, look in a reference book or ask an adult to help you.

Put each feather you collect in a transparent plastic or polythene envelope which will protect your specimen from dust and damage. Mount the envelope on a page of a scrapbook. Another method is to hold a feather in position with sticky tape (as in the illustration).

Next to each mounted feather make a note of the date and the place where you found it. Add the name of the bird, and write a few notes about the bird itself. Where possible, also paste in a photograph or a sketch of the bird which you could cut out of an old magazine or draw yourself.

As your feather collection grows, so you will come to learn more and more about our feathered friends!

MOUNT FEATHER SPECIMENS WITH CUT-OUT PICTURES OF THE BIRDS.

Historic Ships

written and
illustrated by
Peter Stuckey

In this feature you can find out about twelve of the many historic ships which have been preserved around the British Isles. If you get the chance, why don't you go and explore these magnificent examples of the living past for yourself?

THE MARY ROSE

The *Mary Rose* of 600 tons was built at Portsmouth in 1511 for King Henry VIII. She was one of the first ships to be designed and built especially for war. She was very heavily armed, and had high 'castles' at bow and stern so that the soldiers could fire down onto an enemy vessel. For 25 years she proved to be a very successful warship. In 1536 she was rebuilt and up-rated to 700 tons.

On 19th July 1545, a large French fleet tried to attack Portsmouth. The English fleet, including the *Mary Rose*, sailed out to meet them. As her sails were being hoisted, many of those aboard went to one side of the ship and, with her lower gun ports open, she heeled over and sank very quickly taking most of her crew with her.

She lay on the sea bed for more than 400 years until 11th October 1982, when she was raised and placed in a special hall near her own museum in the Naval Dockyard, Portsmouth. Both the *Mary Rose* and her museum are open to the public.

HMS VICTORY

If the *Mary Rose* represents the earliest development of the purpose-built sailing warship, then *HMS Victory* is a magnificent example of the last one before the steam engine completely transformed the fighting ship.

HMS Victory is probably best known as Admiral Lord Nelson's flagship at the Battle of Trafalgar in 1805. She was already an old ship by 1805 because she had been launched at Chatham on the River Medway in 1765. However, she remained in full commission until 1812, when she was laid up at Portsmouth. For the next hundred or so years she served as a static accommodation ship in various capacities. In 1922 she was towed into her present dock in the Naval Dockyard, Portsmouth, having been restored exactly to her Trafalgar appearance, and opened to the public.

HMS WARRIOR

HMS Warrior was the first true iron warship because she was built entirely of iron and not, as were some other ships, sheathed in iron over a wooden hull. She was launched on the River Thames in 1860 and was the first true ancestor of the sleek grey warship of today. Although she was fitted with a steam engine, she also carried full sailing rig, as did almost all the steam-engined ships of her day. *HMS Warrior* is being restored at Hartlepool.

ZETLAND

Built in 1800, the *Zetland* lifeboat is the oldest lifeboat in the world. She was stationed on the north-east coast of England, and during her long service her crews saved more than 500 lives. The *Zetland* was finally taken out of service in 1880 and is now preserved in the lifeboat house at Redcar in Cleveland.

BARNABAS

Barnabas was built as a mackerel fishing boat at St Ives in Cornwall in 1881. She is lug-sail rigged, as were most of the small fishing craft of her day. She has been beautifully restored to full sailing condition by The Cornish Friends of the Maritime Trust, which keeps her at Falmouth, Cornwall.

SS ROBIN

The *SS Robin*, built at Blackwall on the River Thames in 1890, is a typical small coal-fired coaster, dozens of which could be seen all round our coasts up to the Second World War. She was sold to Spain in 1900 and sailed under the Spanish flag for 74 years. Now she has been restored and can be seen in St Katherine's Dock, London.

RESULT

The topsail sailing schooner *Result* was built at Carrickfergus, Northern Ireland in 1893. She is a sailing coaster and ships like her were quite common until steam vessels like the *SS Robin* took over. In the First World War (1914–1918), *Result* was used as a 'Q' ship against German submarines which meant she appeared to be an innocent trader, but she had a hidden gun which was used when approached by an enemy submarine. On one encounter she was badly damaged. The repairs to this battle-damage can still be seen. *Result* is now preserved by the Ulster Folk and Transport Museum at Cultra Manor, Carrickfergus.

ALBION

The Norfolk wherry *Albion* was built in 1898. She is the last survivor of the once large fleet of wherries which traded on the rivers and Broads of Norfolk and Suffolk. With their single great black sail, they could be seen for miles across the flat countryside as they made their way along the waterways to and from farms, mills and factories. The *Albion* is maintained in full sailing order by the Norfolk Wherry Trust at Ludham, Norfolk.

KINDLY LIGHT

The Bristol Channel pilot cutter *Kindly Light*, built at Fleetwood, Lancashire in 1911, represents that fleet of superb sailing cutters which took the pilots to and from ships entering and leaving the Bristol Channel. They were regarded all over the world as the finest boats of their type, and their crews as among the best seamen. The *Kindly Light* is now kept in her own dry dock at the Welsh Industrial and Maritime Museum, Cardiff.

HMS BELFAST

HMS Belfast is a cruiser. She was launched in 1939, just before the start of the Second World War. Within a month of the war beginning, *HMS Belfast* had captured the German liner *Cap Norte*. Later, she was in action against the battleship *Scharnhorst* as well as protecting Allied convoys to Russia. She is now moored in the River Thames near Tower Bridge, London and is open to the public.

WAVERLEY

The paddle steamer *Waverley* is the last sea-going paddle steamer around Britain's coasts. Launched at Glasgow in 1946, she worked mostly on the west coast of Scotland until pleasure steamer services on the River Clyde were withdrawn. This fine ship was then taken over by The Waverley Steam Navigation Co. Ltd. Although the *Waverley*'s 'home' is still on the River Clyde, she usually spends the summer months touring ports around the coast and taking passengers on day and evening cruises.

CAMBRIA

The Thames barge *Cambria* was built at Greenhithe on the River Thames near Dartford in 1906. She was the last barge to work entirely under sail, finally coming out of trade in 1971. She is a fine example of those once numerous coasters and has been preserved by the Maritime Trust at St Katherine's Dock, London.

The monogram at the centre of the title is from a bronze culverine (gun) from the *Mary Rose*. The flag on the left is the White Ensign of the Royal Navy, and the one on the right is the Red Ensign of the Merchant Navy. The anchor with the wooden stock is an Admiralty pattern from the days of sail and the other is a fisherman's anchor.

Famous sinistral Paul McCartney knows how difficult it is to learn to play the guitar 'upside down'.

Are you Gallock handed?
Left-handers are known by different names in different parts of the country. Here are some examples – do you know any more?

Clicky handers	CORNWALL
Kay paws	LANCASHIRE and CHESHIRE
Cuddy handers	NORTH EAST ENGLAND
Kecky or keggy handers	MIDLANDS
Coochy paws	DEVON
Cacky or caggy handers	SOUTHERN ENGLAND
Gallock handed	YORKSHIRE
Scrammy	BRISTOL

Are animals left or right-handed? Apes, who use their hands like humans, tend to use one hand more than the other, BUT they don't prefer the right hand; half use their left hand more than their right, and half use their right hand more than their left.

Are you a

by Brenda Apsley

The answer is 'yes', you are a sinistral, if you are one of the 200 million left-handers in the world today! Between five and ten per cent of the world's population favour their left hands and, for such a large group of people, life can be very difficult . . .

Take writing. Left-handers look uncomfortable when they are writing and years ago when school children used slates and slate pencils, and later simple dip pens and ink, writing must have been a very messy business. Look at a left-handed adult filling in a form or writing a cheque and you'll realise that everyday things are not designed with left-handers in mind.

Until a few years ago, people were sometimes not allowed to use their left hands for writing. At school, pupils were forced to learn to write with their right hands, often having their left hands tied to their sides so they couldn't be used!

Why sinister?

But WHY were left-handers frowned upon? In the Bible, goodness and rightness go together, while leftness is associated with evil. Also, the Latin word meaning 'left' is 'sinister', so everyone came to think of people favouring their left hand as evil and undesirable. For many hundreds of years, 'left' simply meant 'bad', and left-handers were not liked very much.

Even today, when we are generally allowed to

Sinistral?

illustrated by John Paice

use whichever hand comes naturally, life can still be difficult for the one in ten of us who is left-handed. Scissors, pen nibs and can openers are designed for right-handers, as are record players, golf clubs, cricket pads and musical instruments.

If you are a left-hander you'll know all about the problems of everyday life. If you're a right-hander, imagine what it must be like to play the guitar upside down! Try this simple experiment. Using the hand that you do NOT use naturally, try to write your name, hold a tennis racket, or brush your teeth. It isn't easy, is it?

Although most objects are not designed for left-handers, there is a special shop in London called *Anything Left Handed* which sells just that . . . from pens and scissors to a left-handed guitar tuition book. There are even left-handed boomerangs, and greetings cards which open from the left!

Famous sinistrals

The left-handed things which I've already mentioned could have made life a lot easier for famous left-handers like the artists Leonardo da Vinci and Michaelangelo. Paul McCartney of The Beatles might have made good use of the left-handed guitar tuition book! Other famous left-handers include the singer Judy Garland, tennis player Jimmy Connors, actors Danny Kaye and Charlie Chaplin, American President Gerald Ford, and King George II of England.

When Baden-Powell (the Founder of Scouting) was an officer in the British Army, he was sent to Ashanti in West Africa. While he was there he noticed that the local population showed their friendship for one another by shaking their left hands. In Africa, where spears and shields were used in war, it was a sign of great trust to offer your left hand when shaking hands. In this way, you had to put down your shield, and yet leave the other person with his spear in his hand. Some years later, when B.-P. started Scouting, he adopted the left handshake for all Scouts everywhere.

Left-handers have been in a minority since earliest times. How do we know? In caves where primitive wall paintings have been found, hand prints of *left* hands have been found beside the paintings themselves, showing that these early artists painted with their right hands while leaning on their left hands. Bronze Age sickles and scythes were made for right handers.

GOOD FOOD

Riddle-me-Rees

devised by Daphne Pilcher
illustration by Mark Viney

There's something to eat hidden in each of these verses. Solve the Riddle-me-Rees and put your answers in the boxes at the end of the lines.

1. My first is in both me and my
My second's in wheat and also in rye
My third is in both bat and ball
My last's in short and also in tall.

3. My first is in both lamb and ram
My second's in train but not in tram
My third is in both little and large
My last is in ketch but not in barge.

2. My first is in both fauna and flora
My second's in Diane but not in Dora
My third is in both bus and ship
My last is in haw and also in hip.

5. My first is in both she and he
My second's in beg but not in bee
My third is in both pig and dog
My last's in marsh but not in bog.

4. My first is in both lobster and crab
My second's in dull but not in drab
My third is in both top and tail
My fourth is in bucket but not in pail
My fifth is in both they and we
My last is in her but not in he.

6. My first is in both finger and leg
My second's in Margaret but not in Meg
My third is in ape but not in eight
My fourth is in both teaspoon and plate
My fifth is in seat but not in sit
My last is in lights but not in lit.

7. My first is in both bake and cake
My second's in pond but not in lake
My third is in both poke and prod
My fourth's in line but not in rod
My fifth is in both eight and nine
My last is in both signal and sign.

8. My first is in both jump and skip
My second's in eye but not in lip
My third is in both head and hand
My last's in sand but not in land.

Solutions on page 63.

On page 2 you read how Keith Whitfield from Tyne and Wear won a competition to take part in our 'Story of a Stamp' feature. On pages 10–13 you joined Keith and his friend Martin Wolf at Harrisons of High Wycombe where they saw how stamps were printed. A few days later Keith and Martin were . . .

Stamping around Edinburgh

by Ann Moynihan

photographs by the Post Office

The last part of Keith and Martin's action-packed week started early on the Friday morning when they (with Keith's mum!) travelled north from Newcastle to Edinburgh to visit the British Philatelic Bureau.

The Philatelic Bureau is the 'mail order' department of the Post Office. Each time a new set of commemorative stamps is issued, the Bureau receives more than 250,000 orders from all around the world from organisations, stamp dealers and individuals like Keith (and his dad!). The Bureau is computerised to deal with all these orders very quickly.

However, the Bureau does much more than this. Collectors can buy their stamps in many different combinations (more about that later), in Presentation Packs or on specially designed First Day Covers. At the end of each year the Bureau releases a complete collection of the whole year's commemorative issues and, if there's a stamp you particularly like, you can purchase a postcard-sized reproduction of it. Some people collect the postcards, and send one of the Christmas stamps as Christmas cards!

Call in or write

If you live in a large town you may have a Philatelic Counter at the main Post Office where you can see and buy all these products which will have been supplied by the Bureau in Edinburgh. If there isn't a Philatelic Counter near you, you can write to the Philatelic Bureau for information about what is available. The address to write to is:

Department CSA
British Philatelic Bureau
FREEPOST
20 Brandon Street
EDINBURGH
EH3 0HN

No stamp is necessary for FREEPOST when letters are posted in the U.K.

Keith and Martin at the entrance to the British Philatelic Bureau in Edinburgh with the display about 'British Films' First Day Covers.

The British Philatelic Bureau takes orders for mint stamps which are brand new stamps which have not been cancelled with the date and place of posting. It sells loose stamps singly or in blocks or various combinations. The combinations the Bureau are asked for most frequently include:

gutter pairs – these are from the middle of a sheet of stamps with the white margin between them

traffic lights – which are from the edge of a sheet with the colour dots in the margin showing the printers inks

cylinder blocks – which are also from the edge of a sheet but have the printers logo or sign in the margin together with details of the printing process used.

Here Keith and Martin are inspecting a full sheet of stamps before it is 'burst' into separate orders. At each desk the set of shelves can have up to £40,000 worth of stamps. When they were taken through a very thick door into the Bureau's strong room they found themselves surrounded by £5.5 million worth of stamps and year books!

The 1986 Special Stamps

The Stamp Bug Club

When you have a special interest like stamp collecting it is very useful to join a club that helps to keep you informed about what's going on and what other people who share your interest are doing. The Stamp Bug Club is one of the largest junior stamp clubs of its kind in the world.

As a member, you will receive a membership card and six times a year a copy of the Stamp Bug News, a magazine which covers all aspects of the fascinating hobby of stamp collecting.

Write off to find out how much membership costs and how to apply, to this address:

Stamp Bug Club (Dept CSA)
FREEPOST
PO Box 109
Oakwood House
St John's Industrial Estate
Penn
HIGH WYCOMBE
Bucks, HP10 8BR
NO STAMP IS NECESSARY FOR FREEPOST
when posted in the U.K.

The Bureau also supplies sets of commemorative stamps in Presentation Packs in which a set of stamps is packed in a special clear sleeve with extra information about the subject depicted on the stamps.

First Day Covers are envelopes with a special design to go with the stamps. At the Bureau these envelopes and stamps are cancelled with a distinctive first day of issue postmark. The envelopes are then addressed to the customer by this machine.

Many collectors have 'standing orders' with the Philatelic Bureau. This means that they pay a set amount of money in advance to the Bureau each year, and whenever a new set of commemoratives is issued, the Bureau automatically sends the stamps to the customer – no queueing at a Post Office! All these accounts are on the Bureau's computer. Here the Cubs are looking up the entry for Keith's dad's account.

Special Stamp Issues

On this page you can see all the special stamps issued in 1986.

The Post Office Board chooses subjects for special stamps which will:

* commemorate important anniversaries
* celebrate events of national and international importance
* reflect the British contribution to world affairs, in particular to the Commonwealth and Europe, in a variety of fields of activity including the arts and sciences
* show the many and varied aspects of Britain and the British way of life

There are certain 'rules' which are followed which include:

* not having any topic which might be controversial or one which might upset people in Britain or abroad
* no living person, other than Royalty, ever appears on British stamps
* anniversaries are generally restricted to 50 years or multiples of 50 years
* within a year's programme the idea is to provide a variety of subjects for the year.

In 1987 the subjects for special stamps were FLOWERS, SIR ISAAC NEWTON, MODERN ARCHITECTURE, VICTORIAN BRITAIN, SCOTTISH HERALDRY, THE CENTENARY OF THE ST JOHN AMBULANCE BRIGADE, STUDIO POTTERY and CHRISTMAS.

ACKNOWLEDGEMENTS

The CUB SCOUT ANNUAL gratefully acknowledges the assistance of the Post Office in the preparation of this feature, and of the staff of the Philatelic Bureau in Edinburgh in particular.

ALL SQUARE

by Eric Franklin

illustrations by Mark Viney and Malcolm Turner

English is a strange language in many ways, isn't it? Some words are spelt the same but pronounced differently, some words are pronounced the same but spelt differently, and some words have a number of different meanings.

SQUARE

For example, 'square' is a most unusual word. If we say 'everything is all square' we mean that both sides in a competition or game are equal. If we say 'he's a square' we might mean that he is old fashioned, but if we say 'he's square' we are saying that he is honest. If we 'square up' to someone, we are asking for a fight. If you 'square things up' you have balanced things nicely and, if you are given a 'square deal', you are completely satisfied, particularly if your opponent is a 'square shooter'.

Mathematicians will tell you that a square is a regular four-sided figure in which all the sides are equal and all the angles are right angles, but no mathematician can 'square the circle' — only a conjuror can do that! Ah, well, back to square one!

CROSS

'Cross' is a another word with many meanings. A cross is a geometrical figure and a religious symbol. If we are cross we are upset and angry, but if we cross a road we are getting from one side to the other. If you have a 'cross to bear' you are seriously worried. A 'cross patch' is a quarrelsome person, but if you are 'crossed in love' you have probably lost your girl friend. If you are at 'cross purposes' you are opposed to each other. When you 'cross swords' with someone you are going to fight, but you 'cross your fingers' for good luck or to ward off evil.

Having had some fun with the words, let us now have some fun with the square and the cross by combining the two. Here are three puzzles with three different crosses, a Greek Cross, a Latin Cross and the letter X (which is nearly a St Andrew's Cross).

You will see that the crosses are divided by a number of lines. Trace or copy each cross and transfer to cardboard. If you extend the guide lines at the side of each drawing so that the drawing is divided into squares, it will be easy to copy them accurately. Make the lines one centimetre apart and it will be a convenient size.

Carefully cut out the crosses and then cut them along the dividing lines, keeping each cross separate. A Stanley knife or a modelling knife is more accurate than scissors, but needs to be used *very* carefully.

Now try and rearrange each set of shapes from each cross to form a perfect square. When you have succeeded — and it isn't all that easy — try them on your friends. Making one of the squares is a particular brain teaser as you'll need to turn over one or two of the pieces.

It will be more interesting if you colour the crosses, each segment a different colour, and then keep each set in a separate little envelope. With these puzzles you have a bonus: each set will make either a cross or a square, whereas most puzzles will give only one result.

Finally, if you find that you just cannot turn the crosses into squares, the solutions are given on page 63.

TITCH . . . Cub Scout

by Leslie Cecil

ESPECIALLY FOR SIXERS

by Dorothy Kinloch

Headquarters Commissioner for Cub Scouts

illustrated by Peter Harrison

A few months ago I went to a Cub Scout Birthday Party. It was a super affair with lots of mouth-watering food and exciting games. At the end I congratulated the Cub Scout Leader on the excellent organisation. The Leader told me that she had had little to do with the arrangements – the Sixers had planned it all.

I was quite surprised – and then I thought: 'No! I'm not surprised really. It's what I would expect most Sixers to do, as long as they have some help and support.'

Are you a Sixer yet? If you are not, perhaps it won't be too long. However, you must never take it for granted that you will become a Sixer. The job doesn't come automatically because of age or length of service. I used to find it quite a job explaining that point to the Cubs in my Pack when I was a Leader.

If you have been appointed a Sixer, then you can be quite sure that a lot of people were involved in the decision. All the Cub Scout Leaders would have had their say, the other Sixers might have been asked, and it's even possible that all the Cub Scouts in the Pack were able to say what they thought.

What makes a good Sixer?

And what do you think all those people would be looking for in a good Sixer? The boy who is the biggest, or the strongest, or with the most badges? Of course not! They would want someone who is dependable and turns up when he says he will. They would be looking for someone who is reasonably smart . . . or at least someone who makes the effort to tidy himself up when it's important to be neat and presentable. They need someone who is pleasant, helpful and hard working. If you complain all the time, or you don't make much of an effort when tidying up, or you go to Cubs only when there's something special on (and 'forget' when there's jumble to be collected or Arrow work to be done), then you haven't much hope of ever becoming a Sixer.

Baden-Powell used to look for something he called 'stickability' in his boys, and that's what I think Sixers still need today.

Akela will probably have a chat with you before you take on the job of Sixer. Akela will realise that you might be a bit nervous about it. You'll be told about some of the things you'll be expected to do, and you'll have the chance to ask questions. Then perhaps you'll say 'Yes'. At a special ceremony at a Pack Meeting the badge with two yellow stripes will be presented to you in front of the whole Pack. When that happens, I think you'll feel very proud.

A Sixer's Job

And now the real work begins! You are about to lead *your* Six. Don't strut around with your chest sticking out saying: 'I'm in charge!'. Start quietly. Remind the Cubs in your Six that Akela has asked for your help, and you hope they will support you. It's a team effort in many ways.

You will possibly be responsible for the Six box and equipment. You may have to organise a Six Duty Rota. You might collect the subs and mark the attendance register. You will certainly be asked to inspect your own and other Sixes from time to time.

I think your proudest moment might come when you are asked to lead the Grand Howl and break the flag. (Remember! If you have to break the flag you will probably have to get it ready, and hoist it to the top of the flagpole or wherever your Pack flies its flag.)

There are lots of other tasks which you, as a Sixer, might do. You may have to welcome guests, give a vote of thanks, help new boys settle in, organise the Pack Noticeboard, run a game or lead a Cubs' Own Service. You may be able to teach other Cubs a skill at which you are particularly good.

Whatever you are asked to do, try to do it to the very best of your ability. Even if you're nervous, just think to yourself: 'I wouldn't have been asked if Akela hadn't thought I *could* do it.' Remember your Cub Scout Promise . . . and remember B.-P. and his stickability.

Perhaps there will be times when you think you are *not* the best person for a particular job, or that you feel you have too much to do at that moment. Wouldn't it be a good idea to ask your Second for some help? He, too, has been given his special appointment, and must always be involved in the running of the Six.

The Sixers' Council

One of the really good things about being a Sixer is that you automatically become a member of the Sixers' Council. This is a sort of Pack Parliament. It's not quite in charge of the running of the Pack

because the Leaders do that, but the Sixers' Council is an important part of the Pack just the same.

At a Sixers' Meeting you may be asked for ideas for the Pack's programme. You may practise for a craft evening so that you can help the other boys, you may plan an outing or an evening's programme, and you might try out some new games. It's part of your job as a Sixer to play your part at these meetings. Don't be afraid to give your opinion, or to put forward your own ideas and suggestions. Akela and the other Leaders will listen carefully to what you have to say.

Whatever you do as a Sixer, make sure you enjoy all the new challenges and opportunities. Always remember you are helping to train yourself to be ready to play an important part in your Patrol and your Troop when you go up into the Scouts.

Good Luck!

1986 CUB SCOUT ANNUAL
NAME THE FLAGS COMPETITION

Steven wins a Computer

Sixer Steven Braithwaite with his prize computer looking at the Name the Flags Competition in the 1986 CUB SCOUT ANNUAL.

There were 1,500 entries in the 1986 CUB SCOUT ANNUAL '**Name the Flags**' Competition. That's a record number of entries for any Competition we've run. Competitors had to identify a number of national flags. The first letter of the name of each country spelt out 'THE SCOUT MOTTO IS . . .'. The sentence had to be completed with the words 'BE PREPARED'. All the correct entries were put into a hat, and the prizes awarded to the first 22 entry forms drawn.

The FIRST PRIZE of a Sinclair Spectrum + computer with a selection of software was awarded to Steven Braithwaite (then aged $10\frac{1}{2}$) of the 23rd Halifax (St Andrew's) Cub Scout Pack in West Yorkshire.

The SECOND PRIZE of a Sinclair Pocket Television (donated by Timex Corporation) was won by Peter Jordan (then aged $9\frac{1}{2}$) of the 5th/10th Potters Bar Cub Scout Pack in Hertfordshire.

There were 20 Runners' Up Prizes of complete sets of Cub Scout Activity and Puzzle Books donated by World International Publishing of Manchester who publish this Annual on behalf of The Scout Association. The Runners' Up prize winners came from all four countries in the United Kingdom.

By the Way . . .

There were entries for the competition from Cubs in the following *twenty-two* countries . . .

Ascension Island, Australia, Bahrain, Belgium, Brunei, Canada, Cyprus, Eire, Gibraltar, Greece, Hong Kong, Indonesia, Lesotho, Maldives, New Zealand, Oman, Qatar, Saudi Arabia, South Africa, West Germany, Zambia, Zimbabwe.

KEY TO COUNTRYSIDE ANIMALS OF BRITAIN

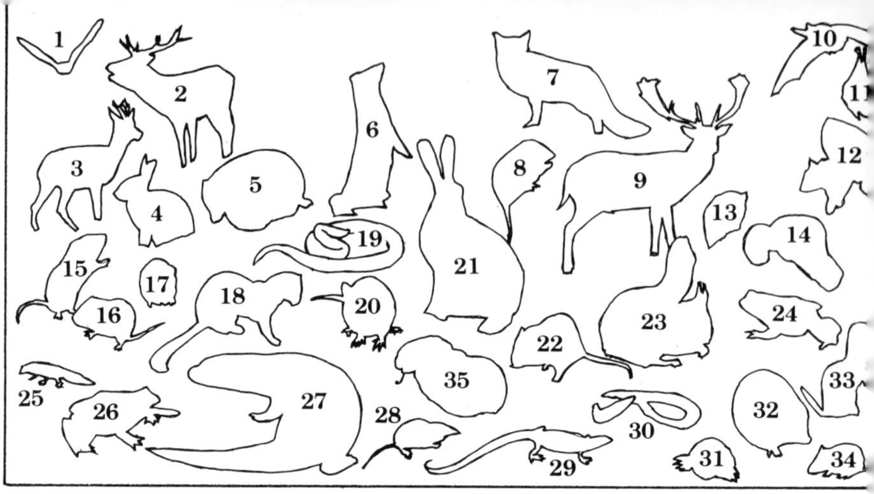

1. **COMMON PIPISTRELLE BAT.** The smallest British bat with a wingspan of about 20cm. Hides in hollow trees or buildings and hunts insects before dark.

2. **RED DEER.** (shoulder height 150cm) Britain's largest mammal. It feeds on leaves and shoots of trees and shrubs. A forest animal which can adapt to the life and diet of the moorlands. Antlers are shed annually until they have twelve or more points.

3. **ROE DEER.** Feeds mainly at night on the leaves, shoots, grass and nuts of the open woodlands. Fully grown antlers have only three points. The spotted fawn is born in early summer.

4. **RABBIT.** Lives in extensive tunnel systems (warrens) usually in grassland or sand dunes. It feeds mainly on grass, bulbs, bark and crops of various kinds.

5. **BADGER.** Excavates an extensive underground lair or set, usually in woodland or copses. Varied diet but savours worms and slugs. Nocturnal.

6. **PINE MARTEN.** Hides by day and hunts in its forest habitat by night for voles, mice, squirrels and birds. Hunts on the ground and in tree-tops.

7. **RED FOX.** Has many habitats and is common in towns. Feeds on rats, mice, rabbits and some fruit and eggs. Despite hunting and persecution, remains numerous in most parts of Britain.

8. **HARVEST MOUSE.** The smallest British rodent at up to 13cm. It lives among long grasses and eats seeds, fruits and some insects. The breeding nest is made from woven grass fixed to grass stems well above the ground and about 7cm in diameter. Now rare.

9. **FALLOW DEER.** Likes woodland mixed with grassland and is often kept in deer parks. The male sports flattened antlers. Eats grasses, herbs or nuts in summer, tree shoots in winter.

10. **COMMON LONG-EARED BAT.** Distinguished by its enormous ears. It lives in buildings in wooded country, emerging after dark to feed on insects which it can catch in flight.

11. **GREATER HORSESHOE BAT.** Britain's largest bat with a wingspan of 30cm plus. It roosts in caves and cellars in winter and forms large colonies in summer in barns and attics. Feeds mainly on beetles and moths.

12. **GREY SQUIRREL.** Introduced from North America in the 19th century and has spread widely through the mixed and deciduous woodland, town parks and gardens of the land. It eats mainly seeds and nuts but will also eat insects and eggs. Can be a forest pest.

13. **COMMON DORMOUSE.** Lives in copses, hedgerows and woodland with shrubs, where it feeds by night on fruits and nuts and sleeps in a nest of twigs by day. Hibernates from October to March.

14. **POLECAT.** Ferret-like dweller in woodland and near rivers, it hunts at night for rodents, rabbits, frogs, birds and earthworms. Moves with a characteristic gliding action. The polecat is hunted as a pest of game and poultry.

15. **BANK VOLE.** Active round the clock, it burrows in scrub, woodland and hedgerows where it eats fruits, nuts, seeds, insects and snails.

16. **WATER VOLE.** Found near slow-moving rivers, lakes and streams, feeding on vegetation in summer, roots in winter. Nests in a hole in banks and is active by day. Often black.

17. **FIELD VOLE.** Blunt-nosed and with a very short tail, it lives under cover in damp pasture and other grassy habitats. It feeds on the stems and leaves of grasses and rushes. In large numbers can cause damage. Active day and night.

18. **STOAT.** Has a tail with a black tip and may become white in winter. Found in many habitats with cover where they hunt for birds, mice, rabbits and hares.

19. **ADDER.** A thick bodied snake of the moorland, heaths and open woodland, it feeds on mice, voles and lizards. It is Britain's only poisonous snake though it seldom bites.

20. **WOOD MOUSE.** Common in woodland, fields, hedgerows and gardens, its diet includes acorns, nuts, grain, bulbs, insects and spiders. Active mainly at night.

21.**BROWN HARE.** Has very long ears with black tips. It lives mainly on farmland with pasture and cereal crops. It does not burrow and the young (leverets) are born above ground.

22. **BROWN RAT.** An Asian disease-carrying species of varying colour, now worldwide due to its close association with man. Eats almost anything and is responsible for widespread food contamination.

23. **RED SQUIRREL.** Lives in coniferous woodland feeding on tree seeds, buds and fruit and the odd insect and bird's eggs. Nests (dreys) are built high of twigs, bark and moss. Very agile and active in daytime.

24. **COMMON TOAD.** Lives in woods, fields and gardens. It shelters by day, emerging at night to hunt for worms, slugs, snails and woodlice. If threatened the toad can inflate its body.

25. **SMOOTH NEWT.** Britain's commonest newt and is found in many habitats. In the spring it migrates to ponds, lakes and damp ditches to breed. Eggs are laid in water and the young are aquatic for the first three months of life.

26. **COMMON FROG.** Prefers damp, shady places and feeds mainly on insects and worms. The eggs hatch as tadpoles and in about three months they have developed legs and can leave the water.

27. **OTTER.** A medium sized carnivore with a long thick tapering tail and all feet webbed. It is found in watery habitats, hunting a variety of fish, birds and other prey. Renowned for its playful habits but decreasing in numbers.

28. **COMMON SHREW.** Lives amid the cover of long grass and hedgerows, feeding on its own weight per day of small animals like worms, snails and spiders. The shrew has a musky smell.

29. **COMMON LIZARD.** Often found basking in grassland, moorland and on sand dunes, it feeds on small animals. If seized it may detach part of its tail and escape. A new smaller tail will replace it.

30. **SLOW WORM.** Not a snake but a legless lizard found in damp areas in fields and woodlands, often under cover.

31. **MOLE.** Active by day and night, it spends nearly all its life underground, usually in pasture or arable farmland. It eats small animals and insects.

32. **HEDGEHOG.** Found in woodland, parks and gardens, it shelters by day and hunts by night for worms, insects, snails and fallen fruit. It hibernates in winter.

33. **WEASEL.** Smaller than the stoat it feeds mainly on voles, mice, small birds and eggs. Small enough to chase rodents into their burrows. Active day and night.

34. **HOUSE MOUSE.** Originally from Asia is now common throughout the world. Eats seeds, grain and almost anything else. Can produce ten litters of five to six young in one year.

35. **GRASS SNAKE.** Slender but can grow to five feet long. An excellent swimmer, it feeds on frogs and newts.

One Good Turn Deserves Another

by David Harwood

Matthew, helped by Mark, adjusts the birds' bag of nuts in Avonlea's garden.

Way back in 1985, SCOUTING Magazine (the monthly magazine of the Scout Movement) ran a 'Your Environment' competition for Cub Scout Packs, Scout Troops and Venture Scout Units. It involved doing conservation projects and generally caring for their environment.

The First Prize for what SCOUTING described as 'a truly outstanding effort' went to the 1st Abbotswood Mohawk Cub Scout Pack of Yate, near Bristol in Avon. But that wasn't the first SCOUTING competition this Pack had won. A few months earlier it was the outright winner of a Bird Box competition, the prize for which was a set of 11 easy-to-construct Malden Timber bird boxes.

The Cubs not only made the boxes from the kits but, under Akela Margaret Williams' guidance, decided to put them to good use in the community. The bird boxes were presented to, and put up in the grounds of, two elderly persons' homes, three primary schools, and two special schools got two boxes each. Akela and Baloo had the last two in their gardens. The Pack's informative scrapbook of their project, complete with photographs, was their entry in SCOUTING's 'Your Environment' competition.

Some months later I wanted to take some photographs of Cubs with bird boxes. I went to Avonlea Elderly Persons' Flats with Matthew Hope (Yellow Sixer) and Mark Summerfield (Green Second) to see 'their' bird box and several others in the grounds.

While we were there, we were spotted by one of the residents.

'Come on in!' she invited the boys. 'Come and see the view I get from my window!'

Matthew and Mark went in, and the lady quickly put them at their ease. 'I love getting up in the morning and watching the birds out there,' she told them. 'The bird boxes and tables attract all sorts. There's always something going on out there.'

Out came the biscuits and the lemonade, and the boys had quite a party! The lady was most interested to hear about their Cub activities, their schools and so on.

When the time came for the boys to leave, the lady said: 'It was so nice of you to come and see me. Do come again'.

So you see, that morning the boys did a good turn without realising it. The bird box had been one good turn and spending a few minutes chatting to the resident was another. Why don't you try something like that sometime soon?

P.S. If you look carefully at the boys' faces you may think they look like two of the three Cubs on the front cover. They are! You see, when I had the chance to take a few Cubs to look over the huge aircraft fire engine at British Aerospace's Filton Airfield, I asked Matthew and Mark to come along with their friend Yazdee Koodabux (the Pack's Blue Sixer). We had a great time! Well . . . one good turn does deserve another, doesn't it?

From the inside looking out and . . .

. . . the view from the outside looking in.

COUNTRYSIDE ANIMALS

Look carefully at the animals on this page. How many of them have you actually seen with your own eyes? How many can you identify? What's the difference between a red deer, a roe deer and a fallow deer? In what sort of place does each animal live and how has each adapted itself to its environment?

We certainly don't expect you to know all the answers! On page 44 you will find a few notes about each of the animals illustrated here. We hope that you'll read the notes and then go on to discover much more about

OF BRITAIN

Look and Learn with Andrex

these – and other – animals by doing some research for yourself.

Studying wildlife is always fascinating. The more you can learn about animals, birds, fish, plants, etc., the more you will come to understand the world in which we live.

ACKNOWLEDGEMENT

This illustration, and the notes on page 44 were first published as one of a set of three Andrex 'Look & Learn' wallcharts by Bowater Scott Corporation Ltd. THE CUB SCOUT ANNUAL gratefully acknowledges the permission granted by Andrex to reproduce the wallchart here.

Andrex

THE HISTORY OF MINTING IN BRITAIN

Coat of Arms of the Royal Mint.

The history of minting coins in Britain goes back over 2,000 years. The earliest coins, mainly imitating continental designs, were made by Celtic tribes in the 1st century BC. Later, during the Roman occupation, a mint was briefly set up in London and this is thought to be the start of the long history of coin making in the capital. This mint only produced coins for about 40 years, and it seems that after the Romans left, few coins were minted in Britain until the 7th century.

By then the Anglo-Saxon kingdoms had become well established, and each Anglo-Saxon king had his own mint to produce his coins. At first the coins carried only an inscription but later the coins had the king's portrait as well.

By the middle of the 8th century these small Saxon coins had been replaced by a heavier silver penny. For the next 500 years these silver pennies were almost the only coins struck in Britain. The problem of giving change was solved by cutting the penny into halves or quarters.

All these early coins were made by a simple hand process which remained largely unchanged for many centuries. First the metal was melted in a crucible and poured into a slab to cool. It was then beaten out on an anvil to a thin plate from which the blank discs could be cut. The blanks received their designs by being struck by hammer between a pair of dies.

Mints were set up in most important towns and at one time there were over 70 mints in the country, but by the time of Norman Conquest in 1066 the number had already begun to decrease and from the early 13th century coins were mainly produced in London and Canterbury.

Medieval coins were made by hand. The metal ingots were beaten flat and cut into pieces. These were then rounded and placed between two dies, and struck with a hammer. Coins were checked for purity and weight before leaving the Mint.

In 1279 the supremacy of the London Mint was confirmed when William de Turnemire was made Master Moneyer throughout England. About this time new buildings were erected for the Mint in the Tower of London between the inner and outer walls, and there the Mint remained, safe and secure, for the next 500 years.

During the reign of Henry VII an important change took place in the preparation of the dies. An engraver now cut the complete coinage design (including the King's effigy) in steel and the coin dies were produced from this original engraving. In this way, a more life-like portrait of the monarch could be made than before when the

A monetary workshop in about 1500.

This view of coining presses in the Tower Mint was taken in about 1809, only a year or two before the move to Tower Hill.

effigy had been made up from small lines, dots and curves.

In 1662 the old method of striking coins by hammer was finally abandoned and replaced by machinery. Bars of metal were now rolled to coin thickness by passing them between revolving iron cylinders which were worked by four horses tramping around a cellar beneath. Blank discs were then punched out of the rolled strips. The coining presses on which the blanks were struck between the dies had two arms weighted with lead which needed four men to turn them.

A press could strike a coin every two seconds, but the effort was so great that the labourers could work for only 15 minutes at a time! The coins struck on these new machines were thicker and rounder than before and it was also possible to give them a milled edge to make them much more difficult to clip or to counterfeit. They were much better than the old hammered coins.

Over the years the conditions within the Tower became very cramped and in 1811 the Mint moved to new buildings just opposite the Tower on Little Tower Hill. The new Mint was considered to be a very modern factory. The greatest improvement was that the machines were now driven by steam instead of by human or animal power.

In the 1880s the factory buildings were altered

The Smirke Building in Little Tower Hill which housed the Royal Mint between 1811 and 1975.

The press line in the Coin Press Room at Llantrisant.

and extended and the Mint continued to keep up with new developments. By 1905 all the Mint machinery was operated by electricity.

As the demand for coins increased, so the size of the Mint on Tower Hill became a problem. When it was decided that decimal coinage should be introduced in Britain, it was obvious that the old Mint would not be able to cope with all the extra work and so a new Mint was built at Llantrisant in South Wales.

As soon as the first stage was ready in 1968, the Mint at Llantrisant began to produce the thousands of millions of new decimal coins needed before Decimal Day in 1971. Minting in London continued until the new factory in Wales was completely finished, and coin production in Tower Hill did not finally end until 1975.

The Royal Mint in Llantrisant uses the latest engineering techniques and equipment to make coins for about 60 overseas countries as well as coins and medals for the United Kingdom.

Weighing newly minted coins.

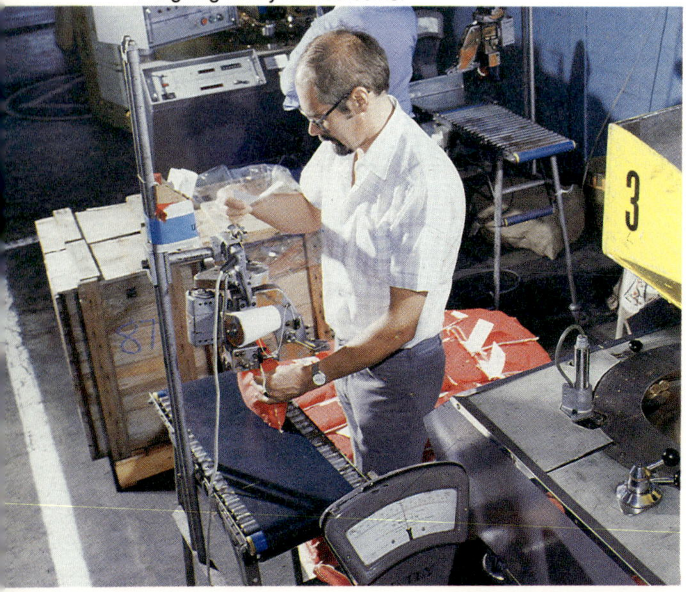

A highly skilled engraver at work on a coin die.

This feature was prepared by the Royal Mint especially for THE CUB SCOUT ANNUAL

A Cub Scout WORDSEARCH

Solve these clues and find the answers in the letter square. The words may be found forwards or backwards, and up, down or diagonally.

1. Baden-Powell was in Mafeking when it was besieged by the ––––– (5)
2. Camper, Collector and Cook are all ––––––––––– Badges (11)
3. You should know, and keep, the Water –––––– Rules when you go swimming (6)
4. You are a ––– ––––– (3, 5)
5. St George is the –––––– Saint of England (6)
6. Wide and adventure games are usually played –––––––– (8)
7. A –––– is prepared for breaking (4)
8. Baden-Powell wrote the book *Scouting for* –––– (4)
9. The first Scout camp was held on –––––––– Island (8)
10. Cub Scouts learn to light a fire and –––– on it (4)
11. Baden-Powell was the ––––––– of Scouting (7)
12. Two of the Founder's first names were –––––– –––––––––– (6, 10)

C	O	B	R	O	W	N	S	E	A	C	R
A	N	E	G	C	S	L	G	A	R	U	Y
N	O	R	T	A	P	H	B	I	N	B	I
R	L	S	F	R	L	I	S	R	S	S	P
B	T	E	R	E	S	F	M	N	R	C	N
O	T	M	L	D	L	C	N	E	S	O	R
Y	L	E	A	N	S	F	O	U	N	U	O
S	A	F	L	U	N	B	N	O	L	T	B
O	U	T	D	O	O	R	S	H	K	N	E
E	B	L	N	F	C	I	L	T	P	I	R
P	R	O	F	I	C	I	E	N	C	Y	T
L	H	N	O	S	N	E	H	P	E	T	S

Solution on page 63.

Make a CUB SCOUT JUNK PUPPET

This puppet was first constructed by Christopher Langley when he was nine years old and a Cub Scout with the 1st Hook 'A' Cub Scout Pack in Surrey. instructions devised by Denise Langley

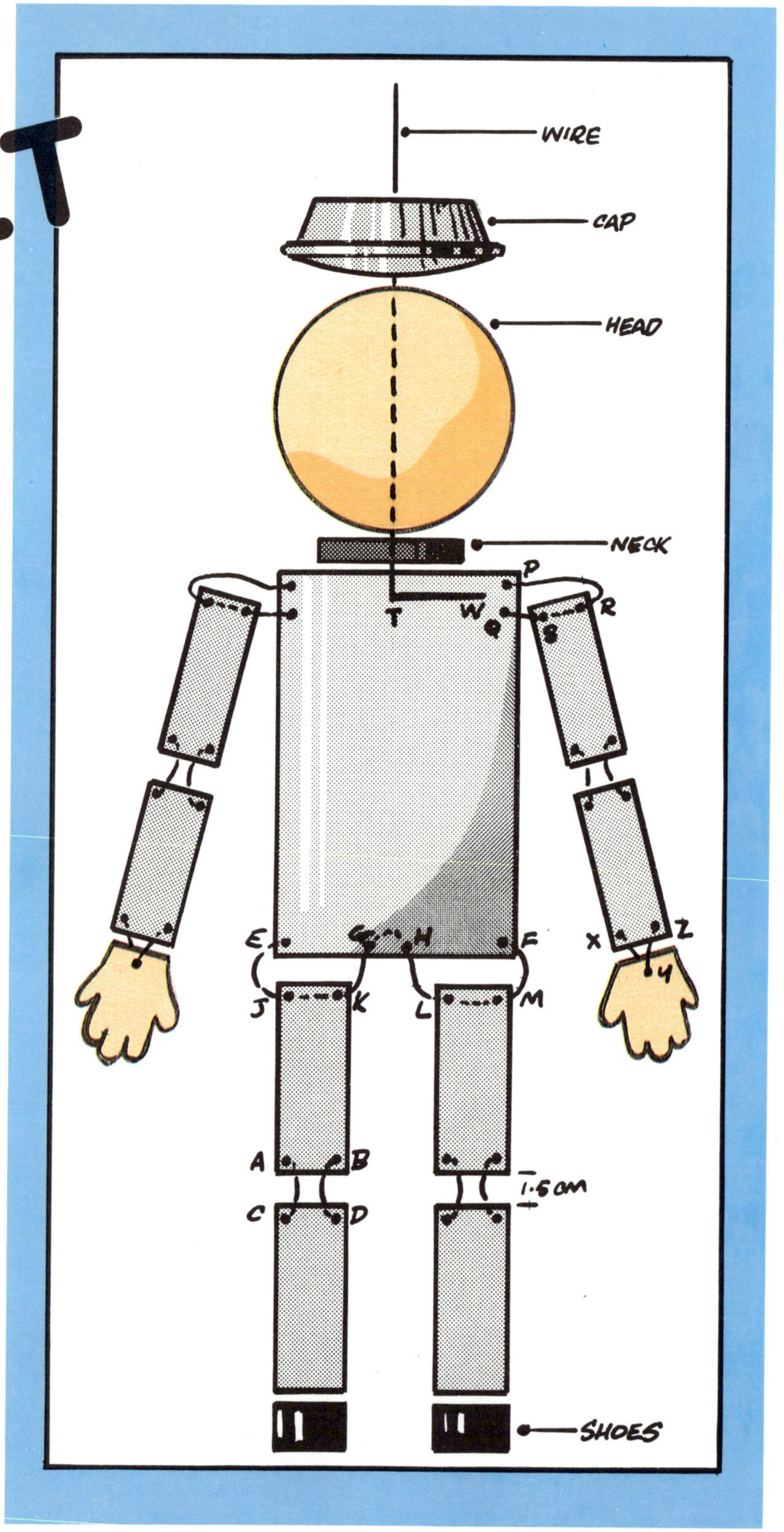

Materials you will need:

8 cardboard toilet roll tubes
cardboard box
(approx 12cm × 18cm × 5cm)
2 small boxes
(approx 7cm × 4cm × 2cm)
2 used foil flan dishes
scrubbed clean (approx 10cm diameter)
old ballcock or rubber ball
(approx 12cm diameter)
wire coathanger
oddments of fabric
grey and green, for uniform
scraps of cardboard
(from empty cereal packet)
paint – black and pink
oddments of wool – black and yellow
scraps of coloured felt for badges
10cm narrow green ribbon
scraps of coloured gummed paper
straight stick or piece of dowelling (approx 25cm)
string
fine cotton thread
glue, skewer, scissors, stapler, adhesive tape

To make the BODY

1. Stand large box on its end and seal all openings except for top flap — cut a top flap if necessary.
2. Cover lower one third of box with grey fabric and glue in place — these are your puppet's shorts.
3. Cover the top two thirds of box with green fabric, slightly overlapping shorts and leaving top *unsealed* with 5cm overlap. Glue into place to make the jersey.

To make the ARM and LEG JOINTS

1. Take two toilet roll tubes and two lengths of string.
2. With a skewer make holes A, B, C and D in tubes, as shown in the diagram.
3. Cut a 12cm length of string. Tie a stopper knot in one end. Pass the 'free' end into A and out of C, and leave.
4. Take a second 12cm length of string. Tie a stopper knot in one end. Pass the 'free' end into B and out of D and leave.
5. Leaving a gap of about 1.5cm between the tubes, put a stopper knot in each string at C and D. Cut off any surplus.

This is your puppet's first leg. Repeat this process three times to make his second leg and his two arms.

To complete the LEGS

1. Paint both legs pink.
2. Take two 5cm wide strips of grey fabric and glue round the top half of each 'thigh' to complete the shorts.
3. Take two 7.5cm wide strips of grey fabric and glue round lower part of legs to represent socks.
4. Take 5cm length of narrow green ribbon, fold in half and staple near top of sock as a garter. Repeat for second leg.

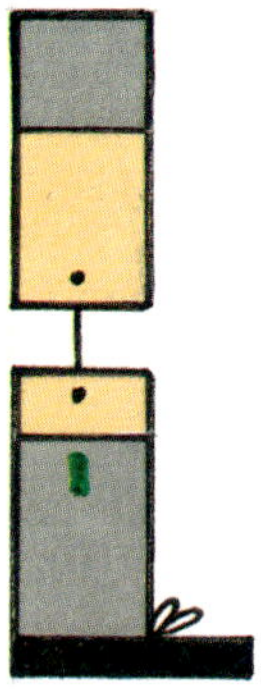

To make the SHOES

1. Paint both small boxes black and, when dry, glue to ends of 'legs' as shoes.
2. Tie bows in two lengths of black wool and glue to shoes at base of socks to represent shoe laces.

To attach LEGS to BODY

1. With a skewer make holes E and F on either side of the body about 1cm up from the base (grey end).
2. Make two holes (G and H) 1cm apart in the centre of the grey box bottom.
3. Make holes J, K, L and M at top of thighs.
4. Tie a stopper knot at one end of a long piece of string and, starting *inside* the body, pass string out of E, through first leg (J and K) into G, out at H, through second leg (L and M) and back into body through F. Allow enough string for legs to swing 1cm below body. Then tie a stopper knot and cut off surplus.

To complete the ARMS

1. Cover both arms (i.e. all four tubes) in green fabric to match body top, and glue.
2. Cut small triangles of red and yellow felt, and glue to left upper arm to represent Proficiency Badges.
3. Cut rectangles of suitably coloured felt for County/District Badges, and glue to right upper arm.

To make the HANDS

1. Trace this hand pattern twice, and cut two hands from cardboard.

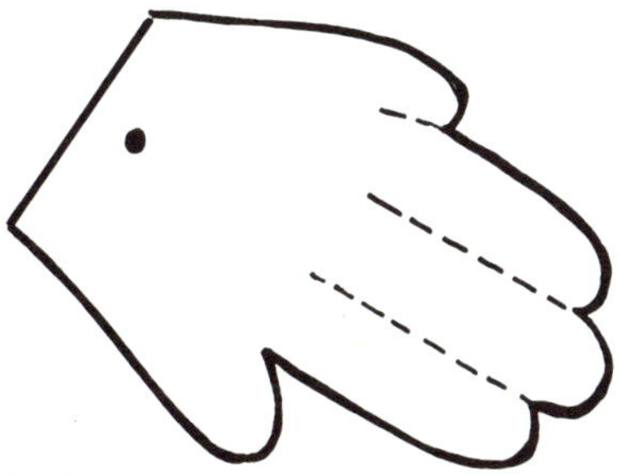

2. Paint pink and, when dry, draw in lines between fingers.
3. Make hole in hand with skewer at Y, and make holes X and Z in tube at wrist.
4. Take a 12cm length of string. Pass through X, Y and Z.
5. Tie a stopper knot at each end of the string, leaving the hand swinging free.
6. Repeat for second hand.

To attach ARMS to BODY

1. Use a skewer to make hole P on the right side of the body 2cm from the top (shoulder). Make hole Q 4cm below P.
2. Make two holes (R and S) at the top of right upper arm in tube.
3. Take a 15cm length of string. Tie a stopper knot at one end. Thread the free end out of the body through P, through arm at R and S, and back into body at Q. Leave enough string for arm to swing freely.
4. Tie a stopper knot inside the box at Q. Cut off any surplus string.
5. Repeat for left arm.

To make the HEAD

1. Use a skewer to make a hole straight through your ball or ballcock from the neck position to the top of the head.
2. Paint the head pink and, when the paint is dry, glue lengths of black wool to the top, back, sides and fringe for the hair.
3. Cut face features (eyes, nose, mouth) from gummed paper.
4. When paint is quite dry, stick features on face.
5. Glue on wool for eyebrows.

To make the CAP

1. Cut circle of foil from flan dish to fit puppet's head, plus small semi-circle of foil for peak. Staple together to make a cap.
2. Cover with green fabric and staple round edges to secure.
3. Glue three lengths of yellow wool across cap making six equal segments.
4. Glue on a 'cap badge' of green and yellow felt to centre of segment above the peak.
5. Bend cap to shape of head.

To attach the HEAD

1. Seal top of body box with tape *leaving fabric unsealed.*
2. Cut 40cm of wire from coat hanger and bend as shown in diagram.
3. Use a skewer to make a hole in centre of body box top.
4. Pass end of wire W into box to support the body.
5. Glue and/or tape at T to secure.
6. Cut two 12cm by 1cm cardboard strips, paint pink and when dry, glue ends to form a circle (the neck).
7. Put neck over wire, then push wire through holes in head and glue head to neck.
8. Make hole in centre of cap, thread onto wire and glue to hair.
9. Bend top 6cm of wire into a hook, and hang puppet up onto your stick.

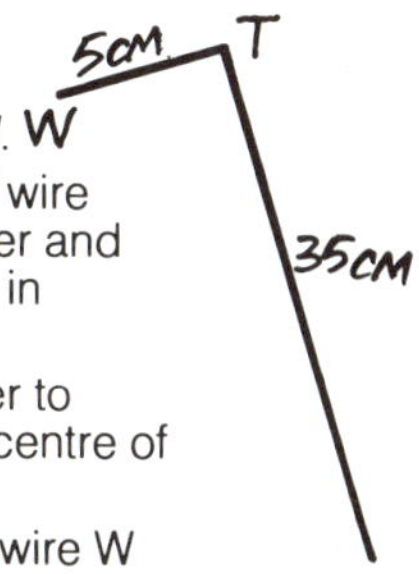

The Finishing Touches

1. Gather and staple green fabric to form shoulders and tuck edges under neck.
2. Cut fabric triangle to make a Cub Scout neckerchief, and secure around neck with a woggle made from felt or plastic piping.
3. A circle of purple felt with white Fleur-de-Lys can be glued to your puppet's jersey – his Scout Membership Badge.
4. Make a hole in the palm of each hand with a needle, and attach a length of fine, strong cotton thread to each hand.
5. Tie the cotton to the ends of the 25cm stick or length of dowelling, and you will be able to manipulate your puppet's arms to make him wave and salute.
6. You could add 'strings' to his feet to make him walk, too!

Helping People who are Blind

by Gill Pawley

illustrated by Marion Strange

As a Cub Scout you promise to help other people and in the Arrow Scheme there are some activities where you can particularly help people with handicaps. You may know of someone with a handicap, or perhaps you may be handicapped in some way yourself. The extent of a handicap can vary tremendously. It could be something quite simple which doesn't restrict a person very much, or it could make a 'normal' life very difficult. The important thing to realise is that there is always something which you could do, but do make every effort to act 'normally' yourself. The last thing a person with a handicap wants is *pity* from other people.

For a moment, let's consider how you could help people who are blind.

Just because a person is called 'blind', it does not mean that he can see nothing at all. For example, some eye diseases mean that it is possible for a person to see something when looking straight ahead, but nothing at all when he looks to the sides. Other people will be partially sighted so that what they see might be distorted or blurred. So, never assume that all blind people live in a world of total darkness.

Close your own eyes for a moment and think what it is like to do some every day things without any sight. How easy would it be to walk from one room to another in your home? What problems might you have getting dressed in the morning?

Some people are born blind, so they have always only had four of their five senses – smell, touch, taste and hearing. Others, through illness or accident, lose their sight at a later stage in their lives. Many people's sight fails as they get older and that is a time when it is much more difficult to adjust and to learn new skills.

In buildings the four important factors for a partially sighted person are LIGHT, BRIGHT COLOURS, TEXTURE and SOUND

When blind people are out and about, they will usually use one of two ways to help them around. They may have a guide dog, or they may use a white cane to 'feel' the way in front of them (the white cane also tells other people that the person is blind or partially sighted).

Getting information

Blind people are just as keen as those with sight to keep up to date with the news and to 'read' books and other publications. There are a number of ways that blind people can get information. Here are some of them:

* Braille is the best known way of reading by touch. It is made up of patterns of up to six very small raised dots. To 'read' Braille, blind people run their fingertips over the dots. The fingertips have to be very sensitive. There are a number of Braille newspapers, magazines and books giving visually handicapped people a real link with the world around them.
* Many people become blind when they are old. It is often very difficult for someone who is elderly to learn the rather complicated Braille system. There is another system of reading by touch called *Moon* which is based on the standard alphabet. *Moon* has large raised letters which are easy to feel, and older people find it easier to follow. Books and magazines are produced in *Moon*.
* Many blind people use tape recorders every day. Tapes can be used by visually handicapped students to record lecture notes. Visually handicapped people use tapes at work and telephone numbers can be recorded on tape. There are many talking newspapers around the country, which are produced by volunteers recording the latest news on tape and sending out copies on cassettes.

* A tape recorder enables a blind or visually handicapped person to communicate with other people. A message or 'letter' can be recorded and sent to friends or relations: equally other people can send recordings to the blind person.

How YOU can help

You will see blind people out and about. If you are walking along a road and meet a blind person, do NOT automatically assume that he or she wants or needs help (especially when with a guide dog!). If you think the blind person does want assistance, ask what you can do. Do NOT pull or push the person along . . . offer your arm so that the person can hold it, and then *follow* you safely.

Always talk to a blind person quite normally, but remember he will not be able to see the expression on your face nor any gestures you may make with your hands. NEVER fall into the trap of talking to someone who is blind *through* an able-bodied person. For example, don't ask a sighted person: 'How is Bill today?' when Bill can not only hear you, but is quite capable of answering for himself. How would you like it if someone tried to speak to you through someone else?

If you and your friends visit a visually handicapped person in their home, remember to tell them what you are doing. Don't just walk out of the room, otherwise the person might be left talking to thin air! Do NOT move furniture or anything else around. If you have to move something, put it back where it came from because the person you are visiting may not be able to find it if it has been moved even a little.

Do some fund raising to help blind children and blind people. Your Pack could try and collect enough money to buy or to train a guide dog for the blind.

Some useful addresses

The Royal National Institute for the Blind
224 Great Portland Street
London W1N 6AA

The Guide Dogs for the Blind Association
Alexandra House
9–11 Park Street
Windsor Berkshire
SL4 1JR

The time foresters fear most...

photographs reproduced by kind permission of the Forestry Commission © Copyright

If we're lucky, we may get a long, hot summer in 1988. If we do, many of you will head for the countryside at some time, and you'll enjoy a walk through woods and forests with your friends or your Cub Scout Pack.

Wherever there are woods and forests, you'll find notices warning everyone about the dangers of fire. And once a forest fire gets a hold it can be very difficult to put out. What's more, a forest fire destroys more than trees. Woodland flowers, insects, birds and animals are wiped out. Their ruined habitat might recover after several years, but for the creatures caught in the fire there is no future, no recovery.

Although the Forestry Commission may have men on duty in fire towers in high risk areas, it does rely on members of the general public dialling '999' if they discover a fire. ◀

The Forestry Commission relies heavily on the Fire Services in fighting fires, but it does have squads of men available in seasons of high fire danger. There is always a forester on duty who can be contacted by telephone to direct operations and advise the Fire Service. ▶

Each year hundreds of acres of woodland, worth hundreds of thousands of pounds are destroyed by fire. The Forestry Commission's information shows that three quarters of all forest fires are started in one way or another by ordinary members of the public. In most cases the fire is due to thoughtless or careless behaviour . . . a match, a picnic fire, a cigarette end. As a Cub Scout you should not be involved with any of those things anyway, BUT you can help because if you see someone throwing away a lighted match, you can tell your parents, Leaders or any adult who is with you.

You might think, as I did, that the summer was the time when the risk of forest fires sweeping across the landscape would be the greatest, but when I asked the

ACKNOWLEDGEMENT

The CUB SCOUT ANNUAL gratefully acknowledges the help and co-operation of the Forestry Commission with this feature, particularly Assistant Environment Officer Carolyn Hurd (West England Conservancy).

Firemen in action fighting a forest fire. One of the Forestry Commission's main defences is a special foam which is piped from a trailer or a Land Rover to form a barrier in front of the advancing fire. Very low concentrations of the foam can also be added to water, so that it covers more ground.

In very bad or inaccessible fires, the use of helicopters is becoming more common. These are used to 'bomb' the fire with large amounts of water carried in a huge bucket underneath. They are also used to transport men with beaters or sprayers to the site of a fire, and to allow the forester to assess the spread of the fire from above.

Forestry Commission, I was told that this was not necessarily so.

In each forest district, the Forestry Commission operate a Fire Danger Rating system by which the 'hazard' rating can be calculated by taking measurements of rainfall, temperature, relative humidity and wind speed and relating them to the state of the ground vegetation.

Except during periods of obviously safe weather like continuous rain, sleet and snow, each Forestry Commission District calculates a Fire Danger Rating for its area each day. The Fire Danger Rating Index goes from nil through low, moderate and high, to extreme.

Although a long, hot, dry summer will lead to a dangerous time, on the basis of information they have collected over a number of years, the period of maximum forest fire hazard is between February and May when the previous year's vegetation has been beaten down by the wintry elements, dried out by frosts and the spring winds, and the fresh spring greenery has not yet appeared.

There can also be a second period of particular hazard in September and October following a spell of several weeks sunshine and drought.

So it's often the Easter public holiday that foresters fear most, particularly when it comes early in the calendar as it does in 1988 at the beginning of April.

The Forestry Commission wants you to visit their forests, to enjoy the peace and quiet and to enjoy the recreational facilities provided. You can help the Commission to preserve them by taking every care when you are out in the countryside ... and extra special care when the Fire Danger Rating Index is high.

FIRE!

When you visit the forest you are in a unique position to help with fire protection. If you see a fire, however small:

1. Get to a telephone, dial '999' and ask for the Fire Brigade. The operator will put you straight through and, of course, emergency calls from public telephone boxes are free.
2. Be ready to describe the position of the fire as accurately as you can in relation to the phone box, public roads or well-known features of the countryside.

The aftermath of a forest fire: a scene of devastation and destruction. If someone had been more careful, this scene would probably have been full of trees, teeming with wildlife. The Forestry Commission tries to prevent fires by maintaining fire traces which are strips of land within the forest which are left unplanted and mowed annually. They also try and educate people like you and me to understand the causes – and results – of forest fires.

CODEBREAKER SOLUTION

THE DIGITAL CODE

(see pages 14 and 27)

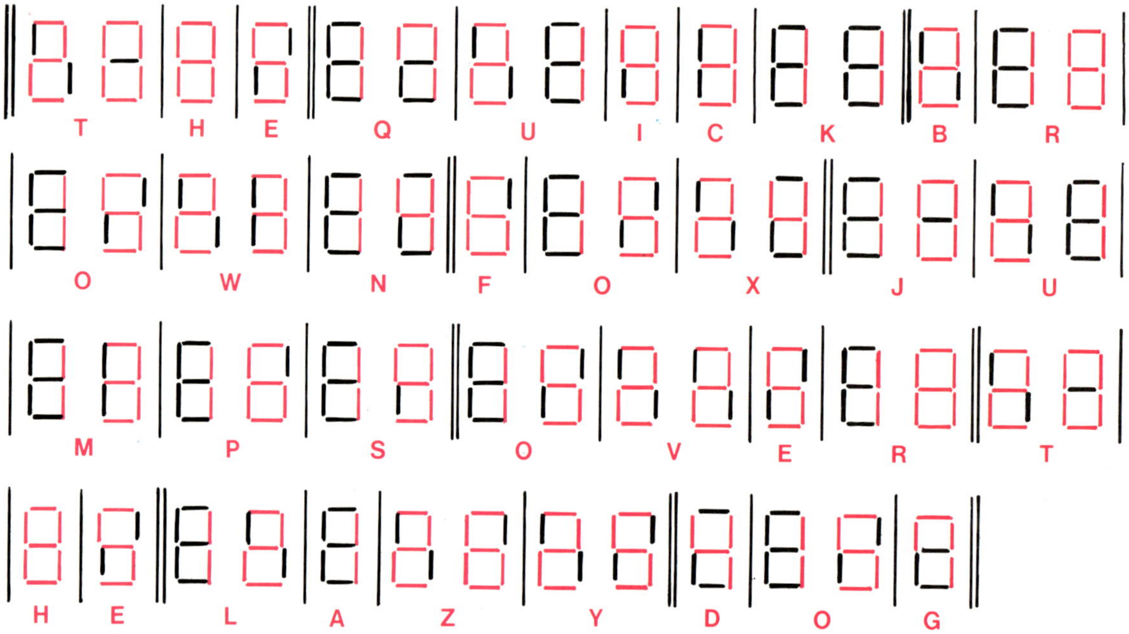

Were you able to crack the code? I hope so, but just in case you weren't successful, this is the whole message with the decyphered code.

Can you see why I've called it the Digital Code? The key to the code is the use of digital numbers. All digital numbers (like those used on calculators, watches and computers) use two or more of the seven lines which make up the 8 like this:

In the code, instead of using the numbers as they appear normally, we've used the parts of the 8 which are *not* used like this:

Then we numbered each letter of the alphabet from 1 – 26 so that A=1, B=2, C=3 and so on.

And that's how it's done!

You can have lots of fun with the digital code as it is, but you can devise your own variations, too. For example, you could give the letters of the alphabet different numbers so A=12, B=3, C=21, or whatever. Whatever key you use, make sure that people who are to decypher your message know how to break your code!

the 1988 CUB SCOUT annual

FREE OFFER

2000 sets of Andrex

'Look & Learn' Wallcharts!

On pages 46 and 47 you can see the Countryside Animals of Britain wallchart. Now, through a special arrangement with Andrex, you could take a trip into the countryside whenever you wish with a complete set of *three* Andrex 'Look & Learn' wallcharts – absolutely free!

The titles in the set are Countryside Animals of Britain, Freshwater Fish of Britain and Trees of Britain. All three wallcharts are beautifully illustrated and cross-referenced to 'Look & Learn' notes. Each wallchart measures 70 cm X 50 cm and is varnished for extra protection and for long life. These wallcharts will look great in your bedroom or on the wall in your Pack Headquarters.

How do you get a set of wallcharts? There's nothing to it. All you have to do is complete the form on page 62. If we have more than 2000 applications by the closing date, all the forms will be put into a sack and sets will be sent to the first 2000 drawn.

This offer really is ABSOLUTELY FREE!

Andrex has given us the wallcharts and the Post Office will be sending them out – that's why you'll find details of the Stamp Bug Club and the 1988 Commemorative Stamp issues in the tube with the wallcharts.

A Cub Scout Crossword

CLUES

1. When looking at wildlife you should be 'as quiet ––––––––– (2,1,5)
2. One of the 'discovering' activities in the Arrow Scheme is to carry out three ––––––––––– experiments (10)
3. When you go to camp you should have one of these between your sleeping bag and the grass (6,5)
4. One stage in the Cub Scout training programme (6,5)
5. You could throw a cricket ball and do the Sargent jump when working for this proficiency badge (7)
6. At this season of the year you may need to feed the birds (6)
7. A member of the Movement who is older than you (7,5)
8. It *sounds* like the good one you should do every day, but, in fact, it's a bird (4)
9. The joint connecting your foot with your leg (5)
10. Cub Scouts should ––––– of others before themselves (5)
11. You can make this with bags or loose leaves! (3)
12. (across) A knot for joining two ropes of different thicknesses (5,4)
12. (down) You'll find one of them in astronomy and astronomers study them! (5)
13. For a 'thinking' activity in the Arrow Scheme, you can ––– or mime the story of someone who has done their best in the past (3)
14. When swimming you ought to know (and keep) the Water –––––– Rules (6)

The Nature Colour-In Competition

THE PRIZES

Overall Winner

This magnificent owl trophy *plus* a cheque for £25 *plus* a set of Portman Building Society 'FOCUS ON BIRDS' prints.

The First Prize
for each age group:

A miniature replica of the owl trophy *plus* a cheque for £15 *plus* a set of Portman Building Society 'FOCUS ON BIRDS' prints.

The Second Prize
for each age group:

A cheque for £10 *plus* a set of Portman Building Society 'FOCUS ON BIRDS' prints.

50 Runners' Up prizes

of sets of Portman Building Society 'FOCUS ON BIRDS' prints.

The natural world is full of colour. All living things use colour in one way or another. Sometimes their colour blends in with the background for camouflage. Sometimes the colours are vivid and bright to attract mates or other living things.

By correctly colouring in the outlines of the six creatures which our artist has drawn on the opposite page, and adding a seventh creature of your own, you will give yourself the chance of winning one of the fabulous prizes which have been donated by the Portman Building Society.

Here's what you have to do

1. Identify and neatly label each of the six creatures shown.
2. Using inks, paints or crayons colour in each of the creatures in their natural colours.
3. Outline, label and colour in a seventh creature of your own choice in the space at the bottom of the panel.
4. If you wish, you can add a general background to the whole picture panel.
5. Complete the Entry Form on page 61 with your name, address, date of birth and Cub Scout Pack.
6. Carefully cut out the Entry Form along the lines shown and send it to: CUB SCOUT ANNUAL COMPETITION, The Editorial Department, The Scout Association, Baden-Powell House, Queen's Gate, London, SW7 5JS to arrive not later than Monday, 1st February 1988.

The Rules

1. All competitors must be under 11 years old on 31st December 1987.
2. Entries will be judged for:
   a. The correct identification of each animal or bird.
   b. The correct colouring of each animal or bird.
   c. The standard of drawing and colouring of the competitor's own creature.
3. Prizes will be awarded as follows:
   a. For the best overall entry.
   b. For the best two entries in each age group:
   * under 9 years old on 31st December 1987.
   * over 9 years old but under 10 years old on 31st December 1987.
   * over 10 years old but under 11 years old on 31st December 1987.

   c. For the next best 50 runners-up.
4. The closing date for the competition is Monday, 1st February 1988.
5. All entries must be accompanied by an Entry Form.
6. Prizewinners will be notified by post before 1st May 1988.
7. Any entry may be published in a future edition of the CUB SCOUT ANNUAL.
8. The Editor's decision is final. No correspondence can be entered into and entries cannot be returned.

This competition is sponsored by

Portman Building Society

The Nature Colour-In Competition Entry Form:

Closing date 1st February 1988

Special Note:

Please make sure you complete this form if you are doing one or more of the following:

* entering the Competition
* having a go at the Challenge
* applying for the Free Offer

To: 1988 Cub Scout Annual
Editorial Department,
The Scout Association,
Baden-Powell House,
Queen's Gate,
LONDON, SW7 5JS

PLEASE COMPLETE THIS FORM IN BLOCK CAPITALS

From:

NAME ______________________

ADDRESS ______________________

____

____

____

CUB SCOUT PACK

____

DATE OF BIRTH ______________________

Please complete this section as well.
The three items I most enjoyed in this Annual were:

1. ______________________
2. ______________________
3. ______________________

I would like to make these suggestions for features in future Cub Scout Annuals:

1. ______________________

____

2. ______________________

Draw your own picture of a wild animal or bird here, label it, and colour it in.

DON'T FORGET THE CLOSING DATE IS 1st FEBRUARY 1988

cut carefully along the dotted line

SPECIAL OFFER (see page 59)

ANDREX 'LOOK & LEARN'

WALLCHART SETS

Please enter my name in the draw for one of the 2,000 FREE sets of Andrex 'Look & Learn' wallcharts. (Closing date 1st February 1988.)

Block Capitals Please

Name ____________________

Address ____________________

____

____

Post Code ____________________

From: Editorial Department, The Scout Association, Baden-Powell House, Queen's Gate, London, SW7 5JS

Get ready for the 1989 CUB SCOUT ANNUAL!

You'll be going behind the scenes of the Otter Trust with these Cub Scouts!

There'll be stories, features, puzzles, quizzes, things to make and lots, lots more . . . including a

GREAT COMPETITION

sponsored by the Timex Corporation with fabulous watches as prizes. THE 1989 CUB SCOUT ANNUAL WILL BE ON SALE AT SCOUT SHOPS, GOOD BOOKSHOPS AND NEWSAGENTS IN AUGUST 1988. MAKE SURE YOU GET A COPY!

THE 1988 CUB SCOUT ANNUAL

Challenge...

FOR CUBS LIKE YOU

Cub Scouts like adventure. They like to be where the action is. I'm sure that all of you reading this have been on exciting camps, expeditions, visits and outings with your Pack, your school, your friends or your family. I'm also sure that on at least one occasion you must have met or seen someone important, famous or special; or you've done something unusual or unexpected; or you've experienced something funny; or you've been present at an important event. Well, if you can look back on anything you've done and say . . .

I WAS THERE!

then this year's CUB SCOUT ANNUAL CHALLENGE is for you!

What we'd like you to do is to send us a description or report of something you've done starting or finishing with the words: 'I was there'.

For example . . .

I was there at the St. George's Day Parade at Windsor when . . .

I was there when Akela was soaked when an elephant blew water all over her at the zoo . . .

I was at Wembley for the FA Cup Final when . . .

I was walking down the High Street with my Nan when suddenly a big black car which had no number plates but a flag flying from a short mast on one wing came towards us. It was the Queen! . . .

Got the idea? Your entry can be serious or funny, exciting or unusual . . . it's up to you.

Your entry should not be more than 100 words long. If you have a photograph, a cutting from a newspaper, or a sketch and you'd like to send that as well, so much the better.

PLEASE MAKE SURE YOU INCLUDE YOUR NAME, AGE, ADDRESS AND CUB SCOUT PACK ON YOUR ENTRY.

Send your entry to arrive not later than Monday 1st February 1988 to:

I WAS THERE!

Cub Scout Annual, Editorial Department,
The Scout Association, Baden-Powell House,
Queen's Gate, LONDON SW7 5JS

Your Challenge entry can be included in the same envelope as the Competition and/or Special Offer forms.

The sender of each Challenge entry chosen for publication in the 1990 CUB SCOUT ANNUAL will receive a £5 token and a FREE copy of that year's Annual.